WIN *at* LIFE

UNLEASH THE VICTORY WITHIN

KD DOCHER

Copyright © 2017 by Keldrick L. Docher All rights reserved.

This book or any portion thereof may not be reproduced or used in any manner whatsoever without the express written permission of the publisher except for the use of brief quotations in a book review.

Printed in the United States of America

First Printing, 2017

ISBN-13: 978-1539737957

ISBN-10: 1539737950

WIN at LIFE

www.WinAtLifeBook.com

DEDICATION

To my inspirational friend and cousin Charkelcy Keyone Docher—you inspired me to write this body of work for the world to see. Thank you for your optimism, faith and perseverance. Your legacy and last name are safe with me, we love you "Jungle".

CONTENTS

DEDICATION

ACKNOWLEDGMENTS

INTRODUCTION

FOREWORD

PART1: DEVELOPING A WINNING MINDSET

FLYING FIRST CLASS	1
THE FIRST DAY OF PRACTICE	5
OPRAH'S HOUSE	9
THE UNCONSCIOUS LIFE	13
WINS AND LESSONS	19
LAZINESS IS A DRUG	29
ELEPHANT TRAINING	37
BURN LIFE'S BOATS	41
FOOTBALL SAVED MY LIFE	45

PART 2: A CHAMPIONSHIP LIFE

ANCHORS & PROPELLORS	49
INVEST IN YOU	55

CLIMBING LIFE'S MOUNTAIN	59
A KID NAMED BOP	65
A RICH JANITOR & THE WILLIAMS FAMILY	71
BRAND YOU	79
WEATHER YOUR STORM	83

PART 3: WHATEVER IT TAKES

I'M BUSY WINNING	87
WHATEVER IT TAKES	95
LOUDER THAN WORDS	101
CONFIDENCE IS A CHOICE	109
ON A WINNING STREAK	117

PART 4: A CHAMPIONSHIP LEGACY

ALWAYS BEEN A LION	123
3 TYPES OF PEOPLE	127
PASSING THE BATON	131
THE TEACHER EFFECT	139
STORY OF A TRUE CHAMPION	143

ACKNOWLEDGMENTS

To my mother—Tammie Shree Docher, thanks for the unconditional love and support throughout the years. You have sacrificed so much so my brothers and I could have the best lives possible. There were many nights when we weren't sure where our next meal would come from, but you always made sure that we never missed one. I especially want to thank you for believing in me—even when I didn't believe in myself. You are my "Why " you always have been and always will be.

To My Father—Kelly Lee Miller, thank you for always being there when I needed you the most and instilling the same work ethic in me, as grandpa taught you and your siblings. I'll never forget the time we sat in the church parking lot—I was only about nine years old and told you that "I'm going to have a better than average life" thank you for not laughing at me, but encouraging me to become the best version of myself that I could be.

To my brothers and sisters—all of you inspire me more than you'll ever know. I wrote this book so you all would have something that you could take and apply to your lives, to get you where you want to be in life. As your older brother, I feel obligated to assure that you guys have all of the resources to live the life that God intended for you to live and I will not stop until I help you get there.

To my unborn—maybe it is in God's plan for me to be a father, or maybe not. But if it is, I want you to be ready for the world. Be the light in everyone else's darkness. Smile often, even if you have crooked teeth like your father. J. Cole said embrace your crooked smile, (he's an artist that makes good music); hopefully he's still around by the time you read this. Know that Daddy is always here and no matter what happens, no one will split us apart. Listen to your mother, teachers and coaches—they will only make this journey called life that much easier.

You never have to be like me or anyone else, run against the crowd, don't follow what everyone else does and be true to yourself. You were meant to stand out not fit in. Understand that in life there is no such thing as losing, you either win or you learn. Don't forget to have fun and enjoy life for the precious gift that it is.

INTRODUCTION

I wrote this book not in chapters, but in four parts and twenty-five sections to make it easier and much more simple to read. It's not necessarily designed to read cover to cover, instead I designed it for you to read at your leisure because of it's short sections and conversational tone.

This book wasn't written because I know of some new innovative way of you obtaining the things you want in life. Truthfully—I'm still figuring all of it out on a daily basis, but the thing I can offer you, is a new prospective in which to see life through. This book is for the under dogs of the world, the people who were never the biggest, strongest or fastest—this is for you. Many of you are on a search to finding a better version of yourself, you seek more from life and strive daily to leave your legacy here on earth.

Success—that word is funny to me. People throw it around so loosely now days, but what does it truly mean? I got tired of the artificial versions of the word and adopted the phrase "Win At Life". Winning At Life is you not quitting when the world tells you no, it's you giving it one last push when it seems impossible for you to move on and last but not least—it's you giving everything you have to every part of your life.

Winning has nothing to do with how much success you have or how many points you score. It has everything to do with your mindset and the lessons extracted from the game along the way.

If you've been trying to figure this thing called life out then I invite you to keep reading and hopefully we can come to a resolution together. I encourage you to share some of the ideas, thoughts and perspectives that I've expressed in the pages to come.

FOREWORD

Words can't express how proud and honored I am to play a small part in something so great! I'm grateful that my friend KD, has the courage to follow his heart in adding value to the world by completing this book "Win At Life."

I honestly feel within my heart of hearts that we all possess what it takes to Win At Life—now recognizing it is an entirely different story! The thing I love about life is that it forces you to search deeper within yourself to find your real truth.

In the game of life, the same thing that makes someone laugh—can make someone cry. What's the difference between the person who laughed and the one who cried?

More than likely, it lies in their perspective—which is the same reason why you can watch a football game and by the scoreboard one team lost the game; but their coach would tell you they still improved in the midst of adversity.

I believe we all know that life is a journey made up of different experiences which shape and mold us as human beings. We've all witnessed people that characterize winning by something superficial or materialistic and end up unfulfilled.

What if I told you that you already possess everything it takes to Win At Life? It's just like that new debit card you received from the bank—it has to be activated. I firmly believe the moment we become cognizant of what we focus on; we then become aware of what we feel and when we become mindful of what we feel, we then become conscious of how we feel and how we feel controls our ability to Win At Life.

It is my prayer that you take the words on these pages and tailor them in whichever way they can assist you on your journey. KD is someone I admire and have great respect for; not only because of what he says, but because of his ability to embrace life and its many encounters and still WIN!

PART 1

DEVELOPING A WINNING MINDSET

A FIRST CLASS LIFE

Here I am on a round-trip, first-class flight from Atlanta, Georgia to Memphis, Tennessee to do some work with a good friend of mine. We're 10,000ft in the sky and a grey-haired man is sitting in front of me snoring like one of my congested uncle's. I boarded the plane before everyone else—received snacks, drinks and many other benefits of flying first-class. To top it all off—it's September 26th which is my birthday!

First class seems pretty fancy right? Well, I guess that depends on who you ask. Some people will say that a seat is a seat, while others will argue that first-class is far more superior to any other accommodation. Today, although I'm grateful for the experience, I can't help but feel a bit undeserving of such treatment. Not that I'm not appreciative for the seemingly free trip. But I haven't reached the first class status in my life just yet. Some of you will say I'm being to hard on myself, while others will admire my courage to speak openly about my experiences. Yes— I've gone to college, obtained a good job and done everything expected of me up to this point. That undeserving feeling stems from my desire to acquire more for myself. Better relationships, finances and a legacy that my family can be proud of.

I know people that would give anything to be sitting in this seat, on this plane, at 8 o'clock on a Monday morning instead of at their jobs. Most people feel stuck in life, but believe that a better life is available to them with the right amount of effort.

You're different—that's why you always have that feeling of discontentment. Most of the people that you know, are happy being stuck and will never change. But you—yes you! Dream bigger for a reason. It's the winner inside of you dying to be set free. The longer that you stay comfortable being stuck, the softer the voice of the winner within will be. If nothing is done about it at some point, then failure will become your interpretation of winning.

The lady sitting next to me told me that the airline upgraded her coach ticket to first class because of the inconvenience they caused her. Her explaining that to me, made me observe one very key component about our lives. We don't have to wait for someone else to come in and give our lives an upgrade—we have the power to do it ourselves.

Man, this flight is bumpy and Mr. Grey head is finally waking up. I hope that by reading this, you realize that I'm not some rah-rah motivational guy or someone with a special group of innate skills or abilities. But I'm just like you, trying to figure out this thing called life.

I know that you have it within you to change your situation, if you want to bad enough. Winning is a mentality that we were all born with, but only a few experience the tangible results of it. You weren't born to stay on the ground—you were born to fly!

"Without courage, we cannot practice any other virtue with consistency."
—Maya Angelou

THE FIRST DAY OF PRACTICE

It was the first day of college football practice. I came into college thinking I was the best thing since sliced bread. My high school team won a state championship the year prior—I just finished playing in an all-star game and was a highly recruited athlete that received a full-ride football scholarship. Before practice, I was excited knowing that I would be amongst some of the best players in the entire state.

As I put on that helmet and laced up my cleats—I felt as if I belonged in that exact moment. After practicing for nearly an hour, there came a session called Oklahoma drill. For those that don't know, Oklahoma drill is a football drill in which two football players stand approximately five feet away from each other in a confined space and hit each other to see who can move one person into the other person's territory. The coach said Docher you're up! I stepped up to the line as confidently as I always had and as I looked up—there was a six foot three two-hundred and twenty pound, muscled up guy that stood across from me.

His head was down and his dreadlocks swayed like leaves on an old oak tree. I was scared out of my mind but didn't show it. When the guy stepped up to the line, coach blew the whistle and all you heard was BOOM!

Now, when I woke up—I noticed that my teammates were over me yelling, KD get up! KD get up! And that's all I remember about that. I was so mad that when I returned to my dorm room, I called my mother and told her—"I'm done with football. The coach was trying to make a fool of me by putting me against the biggest guys on the field, I'm giving it my best and I still can't win," I said.

She laughed and asked—are you finished son? (I don't know if I was more upset by her laughing or the hit). I said yes ma'am and she went on to say—"your grandmother worked hours upon hours, in the blistering sun just to put food on the table for me my sisters and brothers." She said—"your grandfather worked sun up, to sun down as a diesel mechanic, just to put clothes on our backs. I had you at sixteen years old—another child at nineteen and one more in my twenties and still managed to work two sometimes three jobs just to provide for you and your brothers." She said you came from a long line of winners, none of which has ever quit at anything in life. And you're not about to start now.

When she finished, I held the phone up to my ear for at least fifteen minutes. The next day, when I went to practice—I was ready. I put on my wristbands, helmet visor and my favorite pair of gloves. I walked onto the field more inspired than ever. Then coach called for Oklahoma drill and said: "Docher you're up." I stepped to the line and there came those dreadlocks swinging towards me again. He was a lot bigger than me—but I was a lot faster.

The coach said get ready—and just before he blew the whistle, I took off and knocked the guy flat out and kept on running. The moral of the story is this; sometimes there will be things in your life that you fear and if you're not careful, the fear will paralyze you. Don't be afraid to punch fear in the mouth and keep on running. On the other side of that fear—is a life without limits.

"The only thing worse than being blind is having sight and no vision."
— *Helen Keller*

OPRAH'S HOUSE

I WANT YOU TO COME WITH ME ON A JOURNEY. Exactly 55 miles from Mississippi State University is a small town called Kosciusko. In that small town a young lady by the name of Oprah Winfrey was born. We would ride by her childhood home when I was young and I always wondered if I could leave and do great things as she did.

Just down the street from Oprah's house—was a community called Hammond Circle—which wasn't the best of neighborhoods. In that neighborhood lived a young single mother of two small boys. One of the boys was very creative and athletic—while the other was more into blowing things up.

The young mother worked three jobs including Pizza Hut in order to keep the growing children fed and clothed. She later begin dating a guy some time after divorcing the kids father. The guy was pretty cool for the most part but there was one problem—one of the children didn't like him. That didn't last long because he showered them with gifts, candy, and money.

One night as the children were asleep in their bunk beds—they were awakened by what sounded like fourth of July fireworks. After the yells and screams ceased—came a brief calming silence. The young mother made her way into the kids bedroom to ensure they were ok and drove them to her sisters house shortly after. They were just victims of a drive by shooting—no one knows how or why—but it's safe to say that it had something to do with the new guy.

The children witnessed on many occasions the guy physically hitting their mother, they would try to step in between them to stop the fighting—but it never worked. They soon became accustomed to the fighting until one day the younger of the two stood up to the guy and said—"If you hit my mother again I'll kill you". Well, I'm sure you all know what happened next—absolutely nothing at all, he never put his hands on her again.

Years later, the boys weren't so small anymore and the athletic child became really great at sports. At the age of twelve—his mother told him that she wouldn't be able to pay for him to go to college, he would have to get a scholarship if he wanted to attend. This lit a fire under the young man and lead him to break records, win multiple state and collegiate championships. After college he decided to take his talents into the business world—in which he took the same championship mentality and excelled in his career as well.

The young lady with the two boys, was my mother, the boy that stood up to my stepfather was my brother Neil and the kid that won those championships—was me. You see, no matter what situation I've been through in my life—good or bad I've won. It's in my blood—it's why I live, winning to me isn't just about championships or trophies—it's a mentality. One that helps you through your darkest moments and allows you to remain humble in your times of success. I refuse to sit back and let life defeat me—instead I choose to win at life.

Growing up down the street from Oprah's childhood home gave me hope, no—it gave me belief. When I was just a kid I would continuously ask my mother if we could go see Oprah at her house, she would laugh and say "no son, that's her childhood home, she no longer lives there." In that moment, it showed me that no matter the situation or circumstances thrown at me—I could still win.

We all, in some ways, have an "Oprah" near us. Someone that pushes us, helps us grow, and inspires us to become better individuals. All you have to do is be aware, and who knows—maybe one day someone will be writing about how you inspired them with your contributions and accomplishments.

"Control of consciousness determines the quality of life."

— *Mihaly*

THE UNCONSCIOUS LIFE

ARE YOU LIVING AN UNCONSCIOUS LIFE? You know, a life where just being ok is ok—one where you always seem to pull back rather than push forward.

Imagine that your life is a canvas; you have a paintbrush and all the tools needed to create a beautiful masterpiece. You pick up your favorite brush—but let someone else guide your hand to paint a portrait on your canvas. The colors they're using are horrible—you want to change it up—but decide to leave their hand on top of yours—painting a picture that you don't even like. In the beginning, you try to fight it, but soon give up after little resistance.

After finishing the painting, you realize that it is quite frankly one of the worse things you've ever seen. All of a sudden you're upset feeling that you could've done a better job. Every day that you don't pursue your purpose in life, is like letting someone else grab you by the hand and paint the picture of your life for you. Maybe you're asking yourself, how do I know if I'm living an unconscious life?

Well, first of all—why do you do the things you do in your life? What's your reason for living? When you're not in pursuit of your purpose, you'll notice that most of the people in your immediate circle are not doing much with their lives. They've likely been doing the same things, day in and day out for years—never giving back to the community and are pretty happy with being average or below average at most things in their lives.

Have you ever been driving and suddenly come to a complete stop at a red light? While sitting at the light—you drift away into a daydream. It's almost as if you're half-asleep and half-awake. You begin to wonder what your weekend will be like and what needs to get done when you make it home. Suddenly, the car behind you blows their horn and you realize that you've been sitting at the red light longer than you intended too.

That's exactly what living an unconscious life feels like. But the problem is—most people never wake up from that daydream at the red light. They just sit there while the cars behind them pile up and blow their horns—just waiting for them to move. Soon the cars will begin to find ways to get around them. And there they sit—at the wheel of life, consciously unconscious. Watching—but never seeing, hearing—but never listening to the outside world. Like a turtle turned on it's shell—in the middle of the highway—you stay there in a helpless state, until someone like me comes along and flips you back on your feet.

Not once in this section did I say living an unconscious life was a bad thing. If that's how you want to live—by all means, I salute you and wish you nothing but the best. But my guess is—you wouldn't be reading a book entitled "Win At Life" if that were the case.

You may be asking yourself—"How do I live a conscious life?" It's simple, your thoughts align with your reality—so if you don't like your reality—then change your thoughts. Before anyone becomes great at anything (including life) they must practice, practice, practice—by doing what I like to call "mental push-ups." Mental push-ups are like real push-ups; only using your brain—building this muscle takes discipline and dedication. Mental push-ups come in the form of reading books that can enhance your life, listening to educational material and learning from the individuals that you look to as mentors in your life.

Consciousness is a mental state of being, so you must first become aware before you're able to identify if there's a problem. When you're living a conscious life, you separate from those that bring you down and grow closer to those that give your life value. You'll no longer let someone else use your hand to paint your life with—instead, you'll paint it yourself—with as many details, colors and as big or small as you'd like it to be.

A conscious life forces you not to be selfish and think that everything is just about you—but realize that the world is much bigger than you. Ask yourself, "Am I living my life stuck at a red light—while everyone else is in the fast lane? Is my life on autopilot while other people seem to have full control over theirs?" If you feel the need to change things up, then do it. But first, understand why you want to make the change. Many people set goals of going to the gym, or making money—without even knowing why they want to make the changes. To change without knowing why you want to do so, is the equivalent to jumping off of a bridge just because you saw someone else do it.

Don't be naïve when it comes to creating change in your life—consciously make it happen through observation and execution. I will preface the above statements by telling you that living a more conscious life is simple—but not easy—so don't get discouraged when things don't go according to plan; that's a part of life. Get up—dust yourself off, extract the lessons from the problem and go at it again.

A race run well can never be lost."
— Dan Groat

WINS AND ~~LOSSES~~ (LESSONS)

THIS THING CALLED LIFE IS hysterical at times. One minute you're at the top financially, physically and relationally. And the next you're on your hands and knees in your living room on Christmas day—alone with tears running down your face—asking "why me"? That was me after being a star college football player—to having no money in the bank, no career path and trying to keep a smile on my face to give the impression that everything was just fine.

My parents attempted to help—but I avoided them for months. I can vividly recall my father calling every week and me tapping that ignore button because I didn't have the money to give him for my hundred-fifty dollar truck payment. I honestly feel even more guilt about the situation as I sit and reminisce about those times in my life.

Pops and I didn't have that great of a relationship back then—but after going through not speaking to each other for months and sometimes years on a consistent basis—one day I answered his call by accident. But that may have been one of the most memorable conversations of my life. Pops began telling me how he made mistakes from leaving my mother at an early age, to apologizing for drinking so much. Ultimately he wanted us to move forward as men, "stop feeling sorry for yourself son, the world doesn't owe you a dime," he said.

We'd been talking for what seemed like hours and his words cut me deep—I believed the world owed me everything. I mean hey—I wasn't doing any drugs, wasn't involved in gangs and I was in college so in my eyes, "The World" owed me something. Maybe someone reading this is having issues with someone in their lives; it may be a relationship with a mother, father, friend or enemy. I encourage you to reach out to them—one phone call, or text message can change the course of your life as the conversation with my father did mine.

I remember feeling defeated at this point—I had no purpose in my life at that time. One day, I called my mother and began telling her that I wanted to get my CDL license so that I could drive eighteen-wheeler trucks. I was broke—but not beaten and knew that if I could just drive trucks, then I could make some real money and get myself out of my current situation. What she told me afterward was something that I'll never forget.

She said "son you're not going to drive trucks—not that there's anything wrong with it—because our entire family has been doing it for most of our life's. You have a greater purpose for your life and I refuse to let you fall short of that. You need to get back to Memphis and get on your feet; it'll take you about a year she said, but you can do it as long as you apply yourself." That's just what I did—I sold anything that was worth selling at the time, in order to get back to Memphis.

Shortly after that conversation, I was able to land a job with a company that I previously worked for. They loved the fact that I already had the experience and hired me over the phone. Happy doesn't even come close to describing the joy that I felt at that moment—then it suddenly hit me that I would have nowhere to sleep once

I arrived there. I began calling and texting relatives that lived in Memphis—to ask if I would be able to stay with them for a couple of weeks, just until I was able to get on my feet.

Everyone had families and their own problems going on and told me that I wouldn't be able to stay with them. I was devastated yet completely understood each one of their points. I was a grown man, asking to live with other grown men and their families. There I was, once again—down but not out, I had a job just nowhere to lay my head.

Then my mother called a few days later and said, "Son I have managed to come up with some extra money so that you can get a hotel for a few nights—but this is all that I have," I was beyond excited. She sent me the money and I was traveling from Alabama to Memphis in my old beat up truck. It was two-toned black with rust on the hood, I still owed my father money for it. I prayed that I didn't get a flat on the way because I had no money to buy a spare tire.

Upon arriving in Memphis, I looked up hotel rates and quickly realized that if I was going to stay in a nice place—I'd only be able to afford a room for one, or two nights. I had to think of something else fast and began looking for other hotels that weren't as nice—but had lower rates. The hotels were for people that would be staying there for an extended period of time.

I finally found a place for a reasonable price that would allow me to stay there for one week—that's all I had money for at the time. As I checked into the room and opened the door—all I smelled was mothballs and cigarettes. I remember thinking, "There is no way that I'm sleeping here for an entire week." But that's just what I did; I commuted to work and came right back to the same room that smelled like mothballs and cigarettes.

One night there was a knock on my door, as I opened it, I realized the people knocking on the door were my two brothers, Kody and Kelneliuz. They began explaining that they had nowhere to stay and needed a place to crash for a few days. There we were—three young men in a queen size bed, a foul smelling room and the decisions we made that put us there.

Our mother raised us to do right, have the best things in life and she always tried her best to provide the best life possible for us. I began to talk with my two younger brothers, explaining to them that we were on the same playing field in life. Neither of us had much, due to the choices that we made in the past. "I won't be in the same position for long; I'm going to get myself together, take control of my life and one day we'll sit back and laugh about it," I told them passionately.

One week came and went—work was going great, but I still had one more week before I could get a paycheck. My funds were running very low and I called my mother again to see if she knew of anyone that I could stay with for the next week or so until I got paid.

She began saying that her best friend and a person that I considered my Aunt—was in the area and would allow me to crash on her couch for a few days. I was so happy to finally get out of that horrible room and get to a place where I could sleep comfortably and take a real shower instead of a wash up, because the shower at the extended stay hotel was nasty.

My Aunt gave me the directions to where she lived—it was about forty-five minutes from where I worked, which meant driving about two hours a day round-trip for work. That meant more gas and more money that I would have to spend. Nevertheless, I pulled up to the house where she greeted me with a hug as always—she showed me around and pointed me to the couch in which I would be sleeping.

The house was tiny and in terrible shape. She had at least two to three of her grandchildren living with her at the time. It was thirty degrees outside and there was no central heat in the house. The only heat came from the oven and she would leave the oven door open to heat the entire house. If we wanted to get fancy, we would place a fan in front of the oven to circulate the heat throughout the house. I was just grateful to have somewhere to lay my head those nights.

As I woke up the next morning and walked into the bathroom to brush my teeth and wash my face. Just before turning on the faucet, I noticed that there was a giant hole in the sink. I could only turn the water on slightly—if I turned the water on any higher, it would leak through the hole in the sink. I simply made the best of the situation. This went on until I couldn't afford to continue driving two hours a day round-trip to work.

My manager finally gave me a key to the store—to open and close it when I needed to. I was extremely happy about this simple thing—not glad to unlock or lock the store, but relieved that now I had somewhere to sleep.

What I would do is—when it was time to get off of work, my manager would leave first. I would leave soon after and grab me something cheap to eat—usually a dollar double cheeseburger. I would then pull back up to the store—park my truck on the backside, open the door and make myself at home. I remember the icicles that hung from the doorway. I didn't have any covers or blankets—there was only a desk, a few office chairs and some fold out chairs. I would get creative—slide the fold-out chairs together, grab a couple of large towels from my suitcase, cover up and go to sleep as best I could for the night.

One of my greatest fears was that I would oversleep and my manager would catch me sleeping in the store and fire me in my first week. Taking a bath in the sink at my job was one of the lowest points of my life, but somehow I remained optimistic that things would somehow get better for me.

This same routine is what I did for the next week, until one day it was so cold that the heat went out at the store. I slept in my old beat up truck that at least had heat. I would have to wake up every hour to turn the truck on, leave it running for fifteen minutes at a time and continue doing this throughout the night to conserve as much gas as I could. Finally, the day came where the company paid me for the work that I'd done for the prior weeks. That day was one of the best days of my entire life—I could finally get a place to lay my head and cook me a home-cooked meal.

Life has a way of humbling you and this situation changed my life forever. It made me appreciate the small things and forced me to understand that all of the things that my parents taught me were for a particular purpose. It also showed me that sometimes—things do get hard—sometimes things are tough—but as long as you push through those tough times, there will be better ones on the horizon.

As the section title reads wins and lessons—there are no losses in life, every bad situation that you encounter, serves as a valuable lesson for learning and growth. Remember that you get to choose the life you want to live and wherever your life is right now you have the power to change it.

"There is a great volcano sleeping in every lazy individual!"
— *Mehmet*

LAZINESS IS A DRUG

MUCH LIKE TYPICAL SUBSTANCE ABUSE laziness can become a bad habit. Addicts start by taking a hit in the morning, another one in the evening and before they know it—they're addicted to this drug called laziness. In extreme cases, people addicted to drugs—get to a point where nothing else is more important than satisfying their habit. They stray away from family, friends and don't seem to care what anyone thinks about them. They turn down help from others and the little money they do get—goes back into abusing their habit.

Most addicts start off with only a small sample of the drug and before they know it—they're using ten times more. They'll up the dosage in hopes of getting the same feeling as they got the very first time they used drugs—

only to be disappointed when their bodies don't respond the same. Once an addict reaches this point, they either end up badly hurt, or in a rehabilitation center.

Laziness is pretty similar. You'll begin slacking off at some meaningless task; it'll feel good the first time you do it. Most of the time, no one will notice—you may not consciously know it yourself—in the beginning. The scariest part of laziness is a term used in fitness called "progressive overload." This is when one lazy task turns into two—two turns into three—so on and so forth. Typically this is the point where employees get fired; relationships fail and most small businesses begin to struggle, or shut down.

When you realize that your life has a purpose, you operate differently. You must put the pressure to be great on yourself; you can't rely on anyone else to do it for you. I'm speaking to you from experience. I remember when I doubled my salary and bought my dream car. It all happened over the course of six to eight months. The praise began to pour in from everywhere—I was excited for about two weeks, then my mind was looking forward to the next obstacle to overcome in my life. Although I was happy for the accomplishments—I knew there was more to achieve. To everyone else—I was living the life, a young kid in his twenties, making more money than people with masters and doctoral degrees. But to me—I wasn't even close to achieving my goals. I knew that only I could understand the drive and ambition that I had within myself. I quickly understood that my idea of "settling" was everyone else's idea of "making it." One problem with people today is they dream to small, it takes a special individual to understand me talking from this perspective.

Winners believe that everything happens for a reason, while failures think that someone else is to blame for their problems. Nothing good ever happened to anyone who always blamed others for their difficulties. Some parts of life are unfair. No one knows why a child is born with a terminal illness, or why a perfectly healthy young man dies unexpectedly. My advice to you is to control what you can control and learn how to deal with everything else that life throws at you. It all comes down to your morals, values and who you become in route to unleashing the victory within yourself.

You should study success and failure equally. For example: If you grew up around drugs, gangs and violence—then there's no need for you to analyze failure anymore, you've witnessed enough already. If you're on the other end of the spectrum—where everyone in your family has did well, then study people like Tyler Perry who grew up in a physically abusive household—got turned down time and time again before becoming one of the biggest names in Hollywood.

If laziness is a drug, then rationalizing is the syringe. Rationalizing is the number one contributing factor to laziness. Your close family and friends can be the worse when it comes to this—simply because they love you so much and don't want to hurt your feelings. For example, you start working out and your spouse doesn't feel that she needs to and talks you out of it. She begins to say things like, you look fine—I like you just the way you are. While those statements may be true, she's not looking at, if you sit on your butt for the next few years—you'll be forty to fifty pounds heavier and at risk for diabetes and heart disease, all as a result of you looking fine just the way you are.

People rationalize being overweight by saying the food tastes too good. They rationalize being broke by saying that all people with money are crooks. Women justify being with lots of men by saying that no one loved them as a child. Men rationalize cheating by saying their current relationship isn't progressing. Whatever your situation may be, don't fill your syringe with rationalization. Look yourself in the mirror and face "your truth," meaning accept exactly who you are and work to change it if you don't like what you see.

You have to be willing to dig yourself out of the rut of mediocrity in order to win at life. Seriously, I don't care if you have to read a half page of a book before you go to work, another half at lunch and the rest before bed. This is your life and you have to continually challenge yourself to become the best version of yourself possible. Reading two pages a day for a year, is seven hundred and thirty pages. That's four to six books that could potentially impact the course of your life, just as Tyrese Gibson's " How to get out of your own way" impacted mine.

It amazes me how people are quick to say "I hate reading" but when you ask them, are they living the life they desire? The answer is always NO. Self-improvement is not something that you get paid upfront for—no one is going to say, "here's a hundred dollars if you read this book that will help better your life." But the long-term payoff will greatly out-weigh the risk of not taking time to read such material.

We live in a society that is conditioned to keep up with the Jones's and look like the Kardashians. You can obtain all the money and fame in the world and still be miserable. It's sort of like a bodybuilder that takes steroids to gain muscle—instead of working out and eating right. He may have muscles everywhere, but he's weak both mentally and physically. Don't be fooled by "appearance victory." This is when someone appears to have it all together on the outside—but internally the core of their "apple" is rotten. Go after real happiness—not delusional happiness in the form of laziness and addiction.

5 KEYS TO OVERCOMING LAZINESS

1. **WINNING IS HIDDEN IN YOUR HABITS.** What you do on a consistent basis—will soon show up when the time is right. Habits create winners and winners create champions.

2. **DISCOVER YOUR PURPOSE IN LIFE.** Why are you here? If you don't know, its time to figure it out. Don't be like a car with no engine—getting towed through life by everyone else that figured out his or her purpose.

3. **USE INTRINSIC INSPIRATION NOT EXTRINSIC MOTIVATION.** Intrinsic inspiration comes from within. For example: if you know that you need to workout, an individual who's intrinsically inspired doesn't need anyone to tell them—they do it because intangible factors within them pushes them past laziness. Extrinsically motivated people need a reward in order to produce at a high level. This method is short term and is very ineffective to sustain long term.

4. **FOCUS ON LIFE'S POSITIVES.** Many times we close the blinds on our dreams before the sun comes up. Meaning that we focus on the wrong things in many aspects of life instead of searching for the positives in the situation. Sometimes in life, when things are falling apart, they're actually coming together.

5. **KNOW YOUR VALUES IN LIFE.** Values are a set of beliefs and principles that you believe in and live life by. Values typically help you decipher good from bad and right from wrong.

"Contentment is being happy while doing something and Complacency is being happy while doing nothing they're entirely different."
— Adam Smith

ELEPHANT TRAINING

ELEPHANTS MAY APPEAR PASSIVE as animals in a circus—but in the wild, they are ferocious beasts that weigh many tons. They're territorial, very protective and can do tremendous damage. How does the circus train them to walk around in a circle, do stunts and obey the ringmasters every command? Obviously, part of it is for rewards and treats for tricks repeated over and over. But elephants are much too strong and powerful for that to work unless they're conditioned.

The circus gets the elephants when they're first born and small. They tie a rope around its foot and drive a stake into the ground to which the other end of the rope is tied. The baby elephant tries to walk away—but stops when the rope pulls tight. So it walks around in a circle the length of the rope—which is the radius of a circus ring. Within that routine they're conditioned to know that they will be fed, bathed and given plenty of water to drink. The baby elephant grows to be a huge beast of several tons. It can effortlessly pull the steak out of the ground, but doesn't know it—because it's conditioned that it can't.

One day, a fire broke out during a circus. The elephants were panicking and instinct took over. They reared up and roared in fear and pain. They couldn't get away—or pull the steak out of the ground to save their lives from the fire.

It's like so many people that can't get out of the rut of life even when given the opportunity for freedom. That which holds them is only powerful in their mind and conditioning—when all they need to do is walk away to be free.

Our minds and dreams are certainly as powerful as the elephant's physical strength and weight—but how many people can't seize the opportunity for freedom because they don't think that it's possible? I believe we all know someone just like the circus elephants—it's time that you break the cycle of conformity and unleash the person that you were truly meant to be.

"To live, to TRULY live, we must be willing to take RISK."
— *Mandy Hale*

BURN LIFE'S BOATS

YOU MUST MAKE THE DECISION to change the things and people in your life that keep you from winning. To decide means to cut off all other possibilities and move forward with what you're pursuing. When you pursue something with only one outcome in mind—you leave no room for any doubt, or negativity to creep in. We as people have to stop it with the "try" mentality (now I know that some cases are different than others, but you catch my drift) we always talk about trying new endeavors—stop trying and make it happen.

When you say you'll "try it out," what you're really telling yourself is; if this doesn't work then hey—I've already got an excuse for it, not knowing that this mentality could be the very reason why you won't complete your goal in the first place. I'm quite sure that some of you have heard this story before—but for those that haven't here you go.

In earlier times—well before life as we know it, there was a Spanish army of six-hundred soldiers. None of which wore armor—only swords, guns and a warrior's spirit. They wanted to overtake the Aztec Empire of thousands. The Aztecs hadn't lost a war in decades. Captain Cortez of the Spanish Army instructed his soldiers—in order to ensure victory—they would burn their boats and the only way they'd be able to return home was to seize the Aztec ships.

As many of you can imagine, after hearing the amazing speech from the captain, the soldiers were both excited and afraid. Everyone was ready to go to war and fight to overthrow the opposing army. As the Spaniards got closer and closer, you could cut the tension with a knife. Some soldiers weren't sure if it was such a good idea to attack because the opposing military out-numbered them by thousands.

Captain Cortez assured the men that victory was inevitable. They only had two options—either die, or take their boats. I'm sure there were times that the soldiers wanted to turn back—but they stayed the course and proceeded to overtake the Aztec Empire. The Spanish Army took over the boats and achieved victory—all because they gave themselves no other option and committed to the mission of taking over the boats and getting back home.

What in your life will you choose to burn the boat on? Is it a relationship, a career, or a financial boat that needs to be burned? You must be honest—look yourself in the mirror and ask "what is it in my life that I need to be more committed too, or eliminate plan B on?" Most people live their lives at about 70% of its full potential; it's average, that would be a C in grade school. If that's where you want to be—there is absolutely nothing wrong with that.

But if you want the opportunity for an A+ life—you'll have to burn the boats and make a commitment to winning at every aspect of your life. You'll have to embrace the process of evolving into the person that you want to become. This process will surely be one of the greatest challenges of your life—but I can assure you without a shadow of a doubt—that it'll be well worth it.

Those of you that are reading this book are different. To some, you may seem weird, or strange because you've always got an idea, invention, or some crazy plan on how you can make the world a better place.

This book is definitely for you—the dreamers and the doers—not the type of person that basks in mediocrity. But this is for the people that strive to win at life no matter what. "Commitment is doing what you said you were going to do long after the mood that you said it in has left," says Inky Johnson. I challenge you to pick a few areas in your life that you want to be more committed in—burn those boats and don't look back.

"Your talent determines what you can do. Your motivation determines how much you are willing to do. Your attitude determines how well you do it."
                                    — *Lou Holtz*

FOOTBALL SAVED MY LIFE

I REMEMBER IT LIKE IT WAS YESTERDAY, my mother and father got divorced when I was just over a year old. I'd only get a chance to see pops twice a week—which was Saturday and Sunday. I always asked my mother why I could only see my father two days out of the week? She'd tell me that it was because he worked so much and I was in school. I remember this bothering me because I loved and wanted a good relationship with him.

My father is the hardest working individual that I know. He would work eighty plus hours a week and give his all to every company, or person that he worked for. But on Saturday's when I'd come to see him, it didn't seem like we were together that long because all we did was work. Then on Sunday's we'd be in church from nine o'clock in the mornings, until the sun went down.

When I was at my father's house, I would open the fridge and there would be more beer in the refrigerator than soda—as a matter of fact—there would be more beer in the fridge than food sometimes. We kept so much beer when I was growing up that at one point I remember thinking that it was the same as soda. It sounds funny now that I reflect back on it—but I remember thinking that back then. He always told me that I couldn't have a beer and it confused me. I just figured that it was his favorite soda—so I never even asked for it again. I'm almost afraid to say this, but it's truly how I felt at the time. At one point I felt that my father loved drinking more than he loved me. Thankfully, pops changed his ways and the fridge full of beer, was replaced by Coca-Cola.

During this period we had a small house in the community projects—there was always trouble to get into. Everything from gangs to drugs was surrounding me in every direction. Some of my family and friends were either affiliated with gangs, or selling drugs; it was almost like that was the normal thing to do. (Let me be clear, although there were drugs and gangs, it was far from the harsh realities that many others faced during this time.) Something within me never allowed me to go down that road. I would work out daily—playing football, shooting a basketball and playing baseball. Sports was my outlet, it was my getaway, my vacation from reality. Every time that I laced up my cleats and put on that helmet and shoulder pads—it was my retreat. It was the thing that kept me from the negativities of society and gave me something to look forward too.

Sports made me a more disciplined individual by showing me right from wrong—how to achieve goals and more importantly why I should work for what I want in life. So why do I say football/sports saved my life? Well, it's because of all of the previous statements that I've mentioned. Without sports, I don't know where I'd be. Probably in some sort of gang, or better yet in jail—wishing that I hadn't made the mistakes that I made.

I'm thankful to every coach that I've had, from little league, all the way up to the championship teams. It's because of them that I'm a better man today—it's because of them why I do the things that I do and it's because of them that I will do my part to influence a generation of people to become the best versions of themselves possible. And maybe, just maybe—I can help save someone else's life by teaching them everything that sports has taught me.

PART 2

A CHAMPIONSHIP LIFE

ANCHORS & PROPELLERS

IN A WORLD FILLED with superficial people—one must be able to navigate with cautious intent. The search for authenticity is on the rise more than ever—more and more people are reading through the rhetoric and becoming aware of the individuals who are looking to wage an attack on the authentic.

In life, you'll run across people that are propellers and those who are anchors—the difference in the two is vast. Someone that's a propeller in your life—will push you forward in whatever you're doing. They're invariably cheering you on and rooting for you to do great things in life. This type of individual is positive—even when faced with severe problems, they find a way to overcome it.

Someone who's an anchor is constantly trying to bring you down and be negative about everything.

The conversations with anchors should be kept short and to the point. If you don't watch it—they'll transfer their negative thoughts and beliefs over to you. Sometimes anchors are disguised as propellers and come off as if they want to push you forward in your life—but when things get tough—the anchor within is always revealed.

She was "The one". I just finished a disastrous college football season that drained me both physically and emotionally. When you love something, you put your whole heart into it. That's just the type of person that I was. I cherished football—but a defeat in the playoffs crushed me. After the season was over, I began to think about life after football. I thought about everything from—getting married—to having children with my girlfriend that I dated for the last few years.

She called one day and asked me to move to Florida—I was living in Alabama at the time and moving to Florida sounded like music to my ears. I begin to think about moving seriously—but I was so afraid because it meant picking up and moving my entire life for a young lady whom I was poised to marry. Just like always—my mother called and tried to talk me out of it—but I didn't listen and proceeded to sell all of my belongings that wouldn't fit in my Honda. When I finished packing my little car, it was weighted down so heavily—that the back of the car nearly scraped the ground. I didn't care because no one was going to stand in the way of my girl and me.

After the grueling twelve hour drive, I was finally in the beautiful state of Florida. As I walked up the stairs and knocked—the door opened and (it was like the Usher song "There Goes My Baby" was playing). She was standing there—we embraced and I was on cloud nine.

Months passed and things were going great. I transferred my part-time job to the area—the relationship was progressing and I couldn't have been happier with my decision to move there. The only issue that I had at the time, was us working alternant shifts—I worked mornings and she worked nights.

As time went on, I noticed that she began to complain about work quite a bit—so one day I decided to do something special for her. I knew that she would be coming home upset on this particular day and I prepared a candlelight dinner, with two glasses of her favorite red wine. The mood was just right—an ambiance of soft jazz filled the room. Eager with anticipation I looked outside every five minutes it seemed. I heard her car pull up and it was game time! My heart began to beat faster and faster the closer she walked towards the door.

Finally—she opened the door and there I sat—at the table with my beautifully prepared dinner and the soft light of the candles spread throughout the room. She came through the door—walked right past me as if I were invincible and went to the room for the night. I was beyond upset—but didn't say a word; instead, I ate and went to sleep. As you can imagine things started to go downhill from that day forward, but I was still optimistic about the situation.

Bills were piling up and money was getting a bit tight. One morning, as I was about to go in for work, I looked outside and my car was gone. I panicked—called the cops and reported the car stolen. The police called back and told me that they found my car and it was in excellent condition. He then said, "Mr. Docher your car wasn't stolen, it was repossessed." I couldn't believe it, I was in shock and even worst—I had no reliable way to travel to work. The following day I asked her if I could drive her car to work since we worked alternant shifts, "I will return home well before you leave for work" I said.

She argued her points about why she didn't want me to drive her car. I proceeded to walk out of the room and call a taxi to take me to work. The cab cost seventy five dollars to drive me twenty minutes to work, (where was Uber back then?) I paid it and I was off to work. After my shift, I wasn't sure how I would get home. Getting another taxi was out of the question and no one that worked with me lived anywhere close to my area.

While looking for other options—I saw that the city bus would take me straight home for a fraction of the cost of the taxi and I caught the bus back home. Embarrassed to let my co-workers see me getting on the city bus, I walked down the street to avoid them. As we approached my destination, it started to rain. The building in which I lived in was about a mile from the bus stop—I got off of the bus and proceeded to walk home. I felt defeated; my head was down as I walked nonchalantly in the pouring rain for what seemed like hours. A car soon passed me—splashing water on my already wet clothes. As I looked back, I noticed that it was her leaving for work. At that very moment—I understood that she was an anchor in my life holding me back, not allowing me to propel to a greater place.

Soon after that day—I booked the first flight out of Orlando back to Memphis. I went there with my entire life packed in a Honda Accord and returned home with only a backpack and a carry-on suitcase. All of my sports awards and championship rings—gone! My dreams of a happy family were gone, washed away in the selfishness of her actions. You must be willing to discard the anchors that weigh you down and allow the propellers to push you to better places in your life.

"Investing in yourself is the best investment you will ever make. It will not only improve your life, it will improve the lives of all those around you."
— *Robin S. Sharma*

INVEST IN YOU

INVESTING IS ONE OF THOSE SUBJECTS that people tend to shy away from. I'm not talking about 401k's, or real estate—although there have been many people that have prospered greatly from those different avenues of investing.

What I'm talking about is investing in something that has a guaranteed 100% R.O.I. (Return On Investment). And that's pushing in all of the chips on the table and betting on yourself. Life is about taking chances—so why not do something that you have always wanted to do, go somewhere that you never thought possible and become the person that you've always known that you could be.

Invest your time sparingly—don't be one of those people that clocks out from work just to rush home to sit on the couch. All of the prosperous people in this world have the same amount of time in the day as you have—so what things are they doing differently? They invest in themselves; they're up in the mornings well before anyone else is even thinking about waking up. On the weekends—when most people are resting, they're working. They put time into the things they want to do and invest heavily in themselves.

How many books have you read this year before this one? How many conferences have you attended? What skills have you developed that have helped you reach the goals you've set for yourself? What kind of investments have you made in you is the ultimate question I'm asking? If you don't know the answer, there is no better place to start looking than right here and now.

There was a time when I worked for a 14 billion dollar company and was blessed to receive a promotion after years of hard work. The company was required to interview all of the candidates whether they were new, or current employees. As I walked into the office—I shook the manager's hand and sat down. The manager began asking me the typical interview questions and I gave him some standard interview answers. Then he asked, "What are this company's core values?" I rattled off the answers correctly and proceeded to receive the promotion. Walking out of the office, I remember thinking—dang, I know the company's core values and don't even know my own. I had invested so much time into making them a better company that I forgot to spend the time needed into making myself a better person.

Please listen up on this portion. I know that many of you love what you do for a living, but before you realize it, you'll look up and those two or three years with the company will turn into ten very fast. Just make sure that you've invested enough into yourself—so that if they suddenly let you go for any reason, you'll have the skills needed to pick up the pieces and keep moving without missing a beat. If you want to help another individual—you must first do the necessary things to make yourself a better person.

You may be asking yourself why is it even important to think about anyone else when you have enough problems yourself? That's a fair question—but think about how you got to where you are today. Someone opened the door for you so why not return the favor and help someone else do the same. I firmly believe that when someone paves the way for you—it's your job to leave your marks on the road.

"Often it isn't the mountains ahead that wear you out, it's the little pebble in your shoe."
— *Muhammad Ali*

CLIMBING LIFE'S MOUNTAIN

Years ago I had a job working with a temp agency—for those of you that are not familiar with temp agencies, these are companies that help people find jobs. The only drawback is they receive a percentage of your weekly paycheck. They were able to land me a job at a tire Manufacturing Company.

My job was operating a forklift, placing semi-truck tires onto pallets and loading the pallets into the diesel trucks. This was a job that I had during the summer, so anyone that knows anything about warehouse work know that one of the worst times to work in a warehouse was the summer. I worked ten hours a day, for six days a week. They paid me a whopping $7.25 an hour and the temp. service took about 20% of my overall pay for the week. I can remember my first day going to this job—the company was in the middle of nowhere.

As I walked into the warehouse I noticed that I was the youngest person in the entire place. My supervisor was an old guy that smoked cigarettes by the case and had no top front teeth in his mouth. The first day was memorable for me—I met a man whom I now consider to be a mentor to me—his name was Louis. Now Louis was a former college All-Star basketball player and should've been playing in the pros—he had to be about 6 foot 9 inches tall and weighed over two-hundred and thirty pounds.

To most people Louis was a very pulverizing guy just by his sheer stature—but anyone that knew him—realized that he was a gentle giant and would help anyone in anyway possible. He took me under his wing and showed me the do's and don'ts of the warehouse business, but there was one thing that I couldn't figure out.

Why was it that this guy with perfect size and ability was working here in this warehouse for the last decade? That question always puzzled me even to this day, not that there was anything wrong with working at the warehouse—but in my eyes, I looked at Louis as a superstar honestly he probably would have been the next Dr. J on the basketball court. We never talked about that—he never asked me why I was there and I never asked him.

Louis was always a family man—he had three girls and each of them were just as athletic as he was. He would work all day, only to rush home to attend one of his daughter's basketball games, or practices. He would always say, "KD we need to get this work done so that I can leave early, I've got to travel to watch the girls play tonight—one of them may score 30 points." I would laugh it off and get right back to work.

I understood and respected him—from the bottom of my heart. He invited me into his home, introduced me to his family and always helped me out with anything that I ever needed help with.

The warehouse job was getting easier by the day; I learned how to place the wooden pallets on the trucks and how to shrink-wrap the tires before they were shipped out. It seemed as if things were clicking for me at this point—I even got used to making less than $7.25 an hour and figured out that I could work other people's shift to get a few extra hours of overtime.

It seemed like only a month—but it had already been almost a year that I was at that job. While in the break room one day, I was accompanied by a wrinkled face man that looked to be at least seventy years old. His hands were marred and tattered from what looked like years and years of hard work—his skin looked as tough as leather. As I sat down to eat my sandwich, I noticed that he was staring at me while I was eating. I had only saw this guy a few times since working there. Everyone always said that he was kind of crazy and to be honest—I was sort of scared to talk to him in the break room.

He looked up from eating his lunch and asked me "what are you doing here?" (In an authoritative tone). With a confused look on my face—I said "I'm doing the same thing that you're doing here, working to earn a paycheck", he then said "no son, that's not what I'm talking about. People around here have been telling me that you went to college, were great at sports and have so many good things going for you. So again, what are you doing here?" Just before I got upset, he began to tell me stories about the hundreds of people that he's seen come in the warehouse with so much talent and such bright futures—but they got caught up in "the system" as he called it.

After he said that, I finally got it. I was selling myself short and needed to push to higher mountains in my life—that old man sparked something in me that day. I think he saw a bit of himself in me. I finished my lunch, told him thank you and a few weeks later left that job.

Never become so complacent that you're afraid to move to higher Mountains in your life. There will be people that will attempt to limit the vision that you see for yourself—don't listen to them, just keep climbing. The worlds best climbers have one secret to performing well—they never look up until they reach the summit.

Most people that begin climbing mountains—never make it to the top. They get to the midpoint, or rest area and watch everyone else climb the rest of the way up and come back down. They view the scenery from the midpoint—but are too afraid to keep climbing. Don't let anyone stop you from climbing the mountain of life. No matter how long it takes, or how much work you have to do—keep striving to get to the top.

"The past is behind, learn from it. The future is ahead, prepare for it. The present is here, live it."
— *Thomas S. Monson*

A KID NAMED BOP

Bop was a young boy who could never live in the moment. When he was in school—he dreamed of being outside playing. When he was outside playing—he dreamed of his summer vacation. Bop always daydreamed and never took the time to savor the special moments that filled his days.

One morning, Bop was out walking in the woods near his home. Feeling tired—he decided to rest on a patch of grass and eventually dozed off. After only a few minutes of deep sleep, he heard someone calling his name. "Bop! Bop!" said a voice from above. As he slowly opened his small eyes—he was shocked to see a woman standing over him. She must have been over a hundred years old and her gray hair dangled past her shoulders like a tangled blanket of wool.

In the woman's wrinkled hand—was a magical little ball with a hole in the center and out of the hole dangled a long golden thread. "Bop," she said, "this is the thread of your life. If you pull the thread just a little, an hour will pass in seconds. If you pull a little harder, whole days will pass in minutes. And if you pull with all your might, months–even years–will pass by in days." Bop was very excited by this recent discovery.

Can I have it? he asked. The elderly woman quickly reached down and gave the ball with the magic thread to the young boy. The next day, Bop was sitting in the classroom feeling restless and bored as usual. Suddenly, he remembered his new toy. As he pulled a little bit of the golden thread, he quickly found himself playing in a garden. Realizing the power of the magic thread—Bop soon grew tired of being a small kid and wanted to be a teenager, with all the excitement this phase of life would bring.

So again he held the ball and pulled hard on the golden thread. Suddenly, he was a teenager—with a beautiful girlfriend named Tiffany. But Bop still wasn't content. He had never learned to enjoy the moment and explore the simple things of every stage of his life.

Instead, he dreamed of being an adult—so again, he pulled hard on the thread and many years flew by in an instant. Now, he found that he was changed into a middle-aged adult. Tiffany was now his wife and a house full of kids surrounded him. But Bop noticed something else. His once jet-black hair started to turn gray and his once youthful mother—whom he loved so much—had grown old and frail. Bop still couldn't live in the moment. He never learned to live in the now—so once again—he pulled on the magic thread and waited for the changes to appear. Bop now was a ninety-year-old man.

His thick dark hair had turned white as snow and his beautiful young wife Tiffany, had also grown old and passed away a few years earlier. His beautiful children had grown up and left home to lead lives of their own. For the first time in his entire life, Bop realized that he had not taken the time to embrace the marvels of living. He had never gone fishing with his kids, or taken Tiffany out on any dates. He had never planted a garden, or read those great books his mother loved to read.

Instead, he had hurried through life—never resting to see all that was good along the way. Bop became very sad after realizing this. He decided to go out into the woods where he used to walk as a boy to clear his head. As he entered the woods, he noticed that the little acorns of his childhood, had grown into huge oak trees. He laid down on a small patch of grass and fell into a deep sleep. After only a minute, he heard someone calling him.

"Bop! Bop!" cried the voice. He looked up in surprise to see that it was none other than the old woman who had given him the ball with the magic golden thread many years earlier.

"How have you enjoyed my special gift?" she asked. "At first it was fun—now I hate it," he said. "My whole life has passed before my eyes without giving me the chance to enjoy it. Sure, there would have been bad times as well as great times—but I haven't had the opportunity to experience either. I feel empty inside. I've missed the gift of living." "You are very ungrateful," said the old woman. "Still, I'll give you one last wish." I'd like to go back to being a schoolboy and live my life over again, Bop quickly responded. He then returned to his deep sleep.

Again, he heard someone calling his name and opened his eyes. "Who could it be this time?" he wondered. When he opened his eyes, he was happy to see his mother standing over his bedside. She looked young, healthy and happy. Bop realized that the strange woman from the forest had granted his wish and he returned to his former life.

"Hurry up Bop. You sleep too much. Your dreams will make you late for school if you don't get up right now," his mother said. Needless to say, Bop jumped out of bed and began to live the way he had hoped. He went on to live a full life—one rich with many joys and triumphs—but it all started when he stopped sacrificing the present for the future and began to live in the moment.

Enjoy the present—don't wish your life away, because unlike Bop, you don't get a second chance. The future will come soon enough, savor each moment. and live a victorious life.

(Story inspired by Robin Sharma)

Believe in the people that believed in you.

A RICH JANITOR
&
THE WILLIAMS FAMILY

ONE OF MY FIRST JOBS in high school was when I worked as a janitor for the summer—to this day that was the best job I've ever had. Many may be wondering how I can consider this the best job when I was cleaning bathrooms and taking out the trash. Being a janitor was my first "real" job outside of working with my father. It taught me responsibility and the importance of being grateful for the small things in life.

During my time there I met a guy named Larry—he had a funny looking walk and a stuttering problem. Larry loved his job and it was evident by the quality of his work. From cleaning the windows, to waxing the floors, he always seemed to exceed the expectations of his superiors.

I would frequently ask Larry what made him work so hard at his job and he said, "It makes me feel good." Larry loved what he did and although he never made much money, I would consider him a rich man—because he accomplished what he set out to do and felt great about it. Me on the other hand, I wasn't initially happy about working for five dollars an hour and waxing floors—but I loved those paychecks, although we only got paid once a month. Don't be fooled, being rich has little to do with money and everything to do with fulfilling the purpose for your life.

While cleaning the coach's office one morning, I found piles of college football letters that multiple teams had written to me—but I never received. Before finding them, I never knew that anyone paid attention to me playing football, especially any colleges. I was so happy that I called my mother and told her that I was getting a scholarship to go to college, although nothing in the letter said anything about a scholarship—but in my eyes, them even writing me the letter meant that I was a worthy candidate.

My mother was happy, and proceeded to tell me "that's great son, but I am moving to Memphis, Tennessee and your father is moving to Jackson, Mississippi—so you won't have any place to live if you stay here." My heart began to race and I could feel myself getting angry—upset because I was just now starting to gain the attention of multiple colleges—upset because all of my friends were here—upset because I would have to choose between my mother and father.

As a child, I hated those situations and as a teenager, the hatred magnified even more. But I gathered myself and said to my mother, "There has to be a way that I can stay here and still play ball." She told me that she would see what she could do—I didn't know what that meant, but the only thing I knew is she didn't say no and that was enough hope for me.

She called me a few days later and told me that my aunt would be willing to take me in—I was excited because I didn't have to leave my friends, or the thing that I loved most—football. My Aunt, like most of my family, came from modest means. There would be times that I would be asleep and roaches would crawl over my face, causing me to wake up in the middle of the night. There were even occasions when I had to dispose of dead mice in the traps. But to be honest, I didn't care about any bugs or mice, the only thing I cared about was sports—that's all that was on my mind. I lived with them for a while, until I began sneaking out of the house and taking the car. After me taking the car so many times, my Aunt called my mother and pops telling them that I could no longer live there due to my behavior.

There I was—back at square one, not having anywhere to live and not wanting to leave. Weeks passed and Aunt Jackie and Uncle Kennis agreed to take me in—although they had six people already living with them, including my Aunts quadriplegic sister Pumpkin. I'll never forget the conversation that I had with my Aunt. She told me that I could live with them, but if I got into any trouble, she would send me to live with my mother. I nodded my head and said, "Yes ma'am I won't be getting into any trouble." There were seven of us living in a trailer. No one had a room to themselves; I was just grateful that they took me into their home. Shortly after moving in—summer arrived and football camps were starting up. I was settling into my newly found lifestyle.

Sometimes you have to let someone draw the outline

to your portrait before you pick up the brush and paint your picture. That's what the Williams family did for me. It was my junior year of high school and I was a star football player on the team. During one football camp, there was a 6'4 270lbs white guy that was always around. Everyone knew of him and his mother because she would always bring snacks for the team. One day after practice that same guy, (everyone knew him as Big P) invited the fellas to his house to play video games and eat pizza.

That was foreign to me—coming from where I came from, people of the opposite race were very hesitant about who they let into their homes. But for some reason, Big P's family welcomed all of us with open arms. I remember walking up to their house and thinking—wow, the yard is as big as a football field. They were by no means rich or wealthy, but in my eyes, they showed me a life that I wanted to have someday. They bought me gifts as if I were a part of the family. On Christmas, there would be presents for Big P, his sisters Ashley, Courtney and myself. They took me in and showed me things that I had never seen. We went places that I'd never been and they showed me a different side of life than I was accustomed to seeing.

I remember thinking—why are these people being so nice to me? Why are they doing so much for me? Big P's mother Mrs. Dee Ann treated me as if I were apart of the family and I couldn't understand for the life of me why. They helped my parents out with anything they could, (not that they needed help) but I think that the Williams family just wanted to lend a helping hand. As I think back on my life and growing up around the Williams family—there were so many good memories that it's hard to pinpoint just one particular moment.

The only thing that I know is, the Williams family showed me a bigger vision for my life. They always told me that I would go on to do great things with or without sports. At the time, I didn't want to hear about anything unless it had to do with sports—but now I completely understand what they meant. They broadened my horizons, equipped me with the tools that I would later use in life and showed me that to get from where you are to where you're destined to be—you have to help others. You must be willing to put your ego aside and uplift the greatness in others Mrs. Dee Ann would say.

Who in your life has shown you a bigger vision of what your life could be? What person, coach, or teacher has impacted you to the point that you'll now be a better person because of them? If you already have someone like this in your life, appreciate them for all that they do and go on to lead a life of service by helping someone else the same way they helped you. Not to do so would be disrespectful to the people that helped you along the way. And remember, no amount of money will ever make you rich—the feeling that you get by doing what you love and the lives in which you impact is what ultimately makes you rich.

"Consider your brand a life experience."
— Daniel C. Felsted

BRAND YOU

BRANDING YOURSELF WILL set you apart from the rest of the world. Start where you are—maybe you work on a job and want to make yourself more valuable. Just do what I did and make the company "need" you—that's right, create so much value within yourself that it's difficult for them to replace you. In 2014, I was entering my sixth year with a 14 billion dollar fortune 500 company as a business development specialists.

They entrusted me with the task of generating new business into the North Atlanta location—as well as bring in additional revenue to the company. I never aspired to create a brand for myself in the previous six years of working with the company. I was on "auto-pilot" and didn't know that I could do any better for myself. I was new to the area and jumped in headfirst—knocking on hundreds of doors and making thousands of phone calls. I unknowingly began to brand myself as an "Industry Expert" by my peers and customers. The guy that was in the role before me was a great asset to the team and made the company over one hundred thousand dollars over the course of a year. He was able to receive a promotion for his excellence. I knew that I had big shoes to fill and was ready to take on the challenge of making it happen.

Over the course of an eight-month period—I was personally responsible for adding over a half million dollars to the company's profits—all because I did extra work, stayed later and came in earlier. Since I was with this particular company for over seven years, I accidently received the training. I'm sure many of you are wondering what I mean by "accidently." Well, if a child is born in a non-English speaking country and adopted by an American family, raised around only English-speaking people, I think that we can all agree that the child would grow up speaking English. That's what happened to me. I was in the environment for so long that I learned more than some people that were higher up in the company than I was. You can do the same thing—take advantage of the free training that your job offers and use it to your benefit.

For the entrepreneurs out there—you must work especially hard to get your name out to the world. Each step must be calculated—but as bad as you'd like to conquer the world with your ambitious fortitude, you must understand that there is a formula to becoming a successful entrepreneur. You have to create a name for yourself that's recognizable to your target audience and create a brand that is synonymous with winning.

People buy into your brand because they feel like they know what they're getting (hints the reason that most people buy apparel by big name companies) for their time and money. If people don't know about you or your brand—it's your fault, not the consumers. If you have something great to offer the world let's not be afraid to shout about it. Many people post on social media about their brands or message only a few times before thinking their "friends" will be annoyed by it. I challenge you to get your message out. If you have something that will help society progress in a positive way—then get it out by any means necessary.

Never let your story go untold, no matter what it takes you should always be willing to share your story with the world even if some people in your life disagree.

Tell the story from your perspective and not anyone else's. Keep it so genuine with yourself that it shocks you when it comes from your mouth.

Most of the clothing brands, music and movies that you enjoy—many times the reason that you like them is because of the stories behind the brands. No one would want to buy apple's products if all they ever talked about was the technical lingo associated with their products. Knowing that Steve Jobs and his colleagues left the IBM Corporation to start a company from his garage and built it into a globally recognizable brand—is one of the reasons why most people fell in love with that company.

You see—many of us wish that we could do the same thing and each time we purchase one of their products—we buy just a little bit of that feeling. Your story should be so compelling that most people are able to see themselves in it. Don't get so caught up in telling people what happened, rather explain why things happened the way that they did. If you stick to that one simple formula who knows, you could be on your way to becoming the next globally recognizable brand.

"Life isn't about waiting for the storm to pass... It's about learning to dance in the rain."
  — *Vivian Greene*

WEATHER YOUR STORM

THE DAY THAT WE ARRIVED in New York everything felt different—from the way the wind blew, to the way the air smelled. I had never been anywhere outside of Mississippi or Memphis Tennessee at the time, so going to upstate New York was like a new country to me. We arrived on a warm summer day onto a military base called Fort Drum (a short drive from Syracuse, NY).

Weeks later, we started school—met friends and got acquainted with our neighbors. I couldn't help but notice how weird the people sounded when they talked. They never pronounced the "r" in most words, for example: Instead of saying water—they'd say (wat-ta) and instead of hair—they'd say (hay-yuh). The accent was hilarious to me, but on the flip side of things, they thought the way I talked was funny as well.

My mother and her husband were doing great at first—we went on trips and did lots of family related activities that we weren't accustomed to doing. We even got our first dog and mama didn't even like dogs. She named it Diva because it was a girl and always stayed in trouble. One day while my stepdad went off to physical training. My mother made us pack our clothes and drove us eighteen hours, in an old Volvo Jetta, back to Mississippi. She was so upset and only stopped when the car needed gas. I remember thinking—maybe her and my stepdad were fighting again.

Later—she told us "never let anyone treat you wrong. You're worth more than that" she said. We stayed down south for a few days—then drove back to New York. I guess she just needed to remove herself from the situation temporarily. In any case, we were back in New York and the roller coaster of life was back on a level plain again. Diva was growing up fast and quickly became a family favorite amongst my brothers and me.

That year the upstate New York winter was brutal. There was about six or seven feet of snow at a time—with ice blanketing cars, trees and rooftops.

Being from the south I never saw a snow/ice storm—the only storm that I was aware of was a tornado. The thunderous roars of the winter storm kept me awake all night. Hell/ice pounded the doors and windows as if someone were knocking to escape the storm. The next morning we woke up to a power outage and trees snapped in two by the weight of the ice. The president declared a state of emergency for upstate New York—due to the devastation and destruction caused by the storm. Power was out for over a month and the food was scarce due to the un-drivable roads.

Sometimes in life, it's not until you're truly tested that you realize how resourceful you can be. The only heat that we had—in the entire house—was a single burner kerosene heater; which we used to boil bath water, cook with and stay warm. We took food from the non-working fridge and placed it outside in the snow and ice to stay cool. The Red Cross truck came to our neighborhood twice a day, but after a week or so, we were quickly burned out from eating the same thing everyday. This single moment forced us as a family to grow closer than ever.

The point of this section is for you to examine your current situation and understand that some things are out of your control. Life won't tap you on the shoulder and say hey there—I'm about to put you to the test are you ready?

Instead, it sends a storm your way—that will force you to grow stronger and build character like never before. Your storm may not be an actual "storm"—it may come in the form of job loss, losing a family member, or even a divorce. Whatever the case may be, understand that it'll soon pass and there is no need to pull to the side of the road of life and wait it out. You must keep driving through it because when you make it to the other side— the sun will shine on your life brighter than it ever has.

PART 3

WHATEVER IT TAKES

I'M BUSY WINNING

IN LIFE THERE COMES a time where failure is no longer accepted—whether it be with family, business, or even relationships. There are two types of people in the world ultimately, those that embrace change and those that resist it. Somewhere along life's journey, you have to decide which person you're going to be. To change may seem simple, but I must admit—it's not as easy as it sounds.

Imagine there's a giant boulder that you have to push up a steep hill. Six powerful men are helping you push the rock—they each take turns pushing, but never push in succession. It's sort of like you trying to quit a bad habit by using multiple tactics, only to be disappointed when you can't kick the habit. Wouldn't it be a lot simpler to go cold turkey and have all six men pushing the boulder uphill all together? As soon as you've got the boulder almost to the top of the hill—imagine three stronger people pushing against the initial six. The closer you get to the top, the harder it'll be for you to keep pushing. That's what real change looks like; can you keep going through the hard times to get to your destination? If you answered no, then I'd encourage you to examine your reasons for wanting to change. In many instances we find ourselves going through life like it's Groundhog Day. You wake up thinking here we go again—day after day, until each day looks exactly like the other. Seek to live a life of purpose and meaning, not one of boredom and a collection of mundane events.

So the question arises, how do you change or prevent this from happening to you? Social conditioning prevents people from being who they were truly meant to be—they get comfortable within the safety of the herd. You must separate yourself from the pack and make the decision to go on the journey of winning at life alone.

Obviously, there will be many people along the way to help you out, but the initial decision must solely be yours. As you know, on any trip, you must first have a destination in mind, with a clear and concise plan on how you will get there as efficiently as possible.

It seems that we like making things more complicated than they need to be. For example, someone gives you a task and asks that you have it finished by a certain date. Of course, you wait until the last minute to cram and finish something that could've been done days ago. I'll be the first to say; this was one of my biggest problems. Social conditioning and procrastination are the key elements to living a life that you have no desire to live.

I wouldn't want to win the lottery. Yep, you heard me right, I said "I wouldn't want to win it" I'll elaborate shortly. Early 2016 the lottery got up to over a billion dollars. Everyone rushed to the nearest store to purchase a "cure all" lottery ticket. I'm sure many people thought that if they hit it big, they would be able to spend the rest of their lives on some remote private island. For me, the lottery creates a false sense of work and a shortcut mentality—you know—getting something for nothing.

This attitude soon carries over into other aspects of your life like your family, fitness and finances. The thought process may not be true for everyone, but as for me, this is why you'll never see me buying a ticket. What if my kid sees me buying one? Then the waterfall effect begins and the newest generation of institutional dependence is created. You're better off putting that money back into your savings account, or starting your own business.

There's a study out there that shows, about eighty percent of people that hit the lottery, are broke within five to seven years. Why do you think that is? I would argue that it was because they had no idea where the money went. They had no plan, no advisors and were aimlessly spending like a blindfolded person, with a bow and arrow, that has no target in mind.

When you've got a destination in mind—you'll still need fuel to get you from where you are, to where you're going. The fuel has to be your reason why you're making this trip in the first place. I know many people that set out on the journey to winning at life and fell short because they ran out of fuel. Their "reason" wasn't strong enough to keep them on the course during the tough times.

You must have the determination of a mother whose child is trapped on the top of a burning building. Imagine that it's a rainy evening and you witness first hand a five-year-old kid stuck on a ten-story building, the mother is standing on another building about ten feet from the one that her son is on. You're yelling as loud as you can, hoping that someone hears you—but no one's in sight. All of a sudden you see this lady jumping into the air to save her child. No amount of rain will stop her and no self-doubt will limit her from getting to her baby. Her will to get to the other side is far greater than her fear of jumping, falling, or even dying. She'll do whatever it takes to rescue the child, just as you should do whatever it takes to save your dreams.

Some people tell me that dreaming is only for kids and that I'm crazy for coming up with so many outlandish ideas. Many of you once had a dream of what you wanted to be in life when you were younger. But somewhere along the way you let someone take that dream away from you. Maybe your family and friends laughed at you when you told them that you wanted to be a doctor, or lawyer. They made you feel stupid and you changed it to something more reasonable. Don't sell your dreams for someone else's reality.

My advice to you, is not to become one of those people that hates life and anyone else that feels a need to pursue a better one.

Some people desire material possessions, philanthropic ventures, or just want to become a person of influence. In each case—you must have a strong passion for the destination ahead. Be as obsessed with achieving your goals, as a crazy ex-boyfriend/girlfriend is about someone they didn't want to let go.

Ok, maybe not that extreme but you catch my drift. I don't know of one influential person, from Steve Jobs, to Martin Luther King, that wasn't obsessed in some way about their objectives to achieve the goals they set out to accomplish. So why should you be any different than, in my opinion, two of the great innovators of our time? We're in a time where people are more passionate about writing a flawless Facebook status, posting that perfect picture to Instagram, or checking out the latest filters on Snapchat than they are about planning out their lives.

Maybe it's because no one ever sat us down and made us take a good hard look at this thing called life. Honestly, there could be many reasons. It ultimately comes down to you making a conscious decision to take the steering wheel of your life and stay on your path to winning no matter what obstacles arise along the way.

On life's journey, there will be many people that you'll have to tell, "Hold on I'm busy WINNING." The truth is—some people are so caught up in being mediocre that if you don't watch it, they'll hinder you from reaching the greatness within yourself.

When you're busy winning, that's when you'll encounter the most distractions. It seems that everyone is tugging at the hem of your garment when things are going great. It's easy to get distracted from your mission by people and meaningless situations.

There were several people that I couldn't associate with because I was on a path to something even greater than I could imagine myself. Hold on I'm busy winning is you telling people that aren't doing the things that you're doing, or going the places that you're going—you have no time for them. Your time is precious and you can't get yesterday back. I encourage you to be smart with your hours, minutes and seconds. One day you'll look back and be thankful that you told those negative people—hold on I'm busy winning.

5 KEYS TO DEVELOPING A WINNING FORMULA

1. **Be Passionate about your goal.** You have to get emotionally involved with reaching your destination and understand that winning happens when preparation meets hard work.

2. **Vision.** How big would you dream, if you knew that you couldn't fail? Aim high but understand that you must endure the process before those dreams become a reality.

3. **Stand Strong in your beliefs.** Stand for something, or fall for anything. Your mentality will be your most valuable tool as it pertains to winning—if you don't have a winning mindset then you will not win.

4. **Commitment.** Adopt a no matter what mentality. Whatever happens you must believe there's a way to overcome any obstacle. (Burn The Boats)

5. **Will over Skill.** Your desire and will to win means everything. Skill is over-rated unless coupled with will. Don't Quit.

What's stopping you from doing everything that you've dreamed of?

WHATEVER IT TAKES

On your journey to winning at life you will encounter many obstacles that will attempt to hold you back from becoming the best version of yourself possible. You must always listen to your heart—it will guide you through some of your toughest obstacles in life. I know that some of you are probably asking yourselves; KD what do you mean listen to your heart and let it guide you? Some people call it their soul or even their intuition, but I call it your heart. That sounds crazy, right? Wrong, only the people that have a genuine desire to be more, do more and want to win at life will be able to understand the concept of listening to your heart.

As I've already stated previously in this book, everything that you're looking for, is looking for you—but you must be willing to listen to your heart and be aware of the signs all around you. There was a time when I lived in Memphis, Tennessee and finally settled into my career. After a year and a half of being in the same position, making the same income and living the same lifestyle—I wanted a change. Residing in Atlanta had always been something that I desired at the time. I can remember looking up places to live in the Atlanta area, two to three years before moving there. After being turned down on five separate occasions for promotions on my job —I listened to my heart as I kept having dreams about moving to Atlanta.

There was no logical reason for me to go there. I didn't know many people, or have any particular network there—so in my eyes, me having these dreams about moving to the big city were irrelevant since I didn't know how I was going to make the dream a reality.

Weeks passed, the dreams of moving to the big city reoccurred day after day. I continued to be curious, saying to myself things like what if this happens? What if that happens? Or what if I get down there and it's the worst decision that I ever made?

I've learned that many times—your destiny lies right on the other side of the negative thoughts and fears that you have of doing the thing you fear. Being the stubborn guy that I am—I ignored those negative thoughts that were in my head and proceeded to look for jobs in the Atlanta area. Each time that I looked for jobs previously—there were never any openings in the Atlanta area.

One day I looked and there were five different openings; I applied for all of them. Not only did I apply for the jobs, but I also followed up on them each day. I understood that there would be multiple people applying for each of these positions and I also knew that unless I did something different than most of the applicants—I would be grouped into the same category as the other individuals. I found the supervisors information and contacted each one via phone/email—and told them that I would like to meet them face-to-face if at all possible. The one thing that I knew was—if I met these guys in person and let them see my personality as well as my commitment to fulfilling an obligation—there was no doubt in my mind that I would indeed get the position.

I packed up my beat up Dodge Dakota truck and was off to Georgia. As I arrived at my first meeting—the manager was full of energy and welcomed me. After talking to him for only a few moments, I knew that I wanted to work with him. Some peoples energy is infectious and after being around them, you have no choice but to consume that same energy—that's precisely what this guy made me feel like. After talking to him for nearly forty-five minutes—about life, the company and why I wanted to move down to Atlanta; he told me that all of his positions were filled.

Walking out of that door I can remember thinking "Man that was a waste of an hour of my life." I started on the way to my next meeting with a different manager and boy do I mean different. This guy wasn't at all like the first gentleman—he didn't have an ounce of personality and for whatever reason—seemed to be mad about something.

After talking to him within the first five minutes—I knew that I didn't want to work with him at all. The meeting was so bad that I called my family afterwards and told them that there was no way at all that I would work with that guy. Upon leaving my second meeting, I was upset because I had driven over six hours—only to be told that there were no positions available.

As I drove back to Memphis (thankfully nothing happened with my truck) and those negative thoughts began creeping in my head.

Then my phone rang—it was one of the hiring managers from the store that I just left, he went on to say that he wanted me to turn around and perform a second interview. I told him that I was already more than halfway home and wouldn't be able to turn around for a second interview. He then insisted that I complete an over the phone interview at that very moment. The manager went on for over thirty minutes—asking me the same generic interview questions—everything from why do I want the position? To what would I do if I caught someone stealing? After the phone interview, he then offered me a position in Atlanta and I gladly accepted.

In closing, remember that there will always be significant conflicts between your head and your heart—when in doubt follow your heart. You may be asking yourself, how will you know what to listen for? Well, it's different for everyone. It could come by listening to another person, in the form of a dream, or by reading a book. However you get the message—listen to it, follow it and never deviate from the path in which it takes you. You must do whatever it takes to get to the place you want to be in life. The moment that you stop listening to your heart/inner-voice—is the moment that you settle for mediocrity and a mundane existence.

"Fear is an illusion, Action is reality."

LOUDER THAN WORDS

MOTIVATION CAN GET YOU STARTED, but it's action that gets you across the finish line. You can listen to as many motivational speakers, teachers, coaches and business partners, as you want—but it's not until you take clear and consistent action on the thing that you plan to do that you'll reap the rewards. This book has given you many different principles, methods and strategies on living a winning life.

I promise that none of that means a thing if you don't get up and take aggressive action. How many times have you heard someone say they'd like to have six-pack abs, or a slimmer waist—yet they never go to the gym, or eat right? If you don't practice the fitness lifestyle needed to make that flat stomach happen, then you can kiss that six-pack goodbye. And the same is true about your life.

The only way for you to get the life and body that you want is to engage in effective daily action.

Many people have a "lottery mentality" and expect everything to happen all at once. They want to hit it big one time for all the marbles and live happily ever after. Although it sounds great—that's an irrational way of thinking. I challenge you not to have the lottery mentality—instead adopt the farmer's mindset. When it comes to your life—cultivate and plant good seeds on good soil.

Be sure to remove all of the weeds in your life which are the negative people and naysayers. Water and nurture the garden of your mind by reading and listening to various informative resources, as well as, associate with like-minded positive people. Make sure that you're as patient as the farmer is after they plant their crops. Much like the farmer—things rarely ever happen overnight. You can't plant a seed one day—come back the next and have a fully grown garden; that's not how life works.

As bad as we'd like things to happen that way and as bad as this "microwave society" wants everything instantly— that is not the way of life. Life is composed of seasons and each season carries with it a unique gift. There's no moon without the sun, or good without evil. You must be prepared and understand that every day won't be the best day of your life. That's not how this thing works.

You're going to have good and bad days. There will be days that you'll be sick and others where you'll feel better than ever before. My advice to you is to take advantage of those good days when you have them and learn how to deal with the bad days when they come—and oh yeah, they definitely will come. A wise man told me—things are going to happen no matter what, but it's the way that you respond to the things that have happened, which will determine the type of person you'll become. I believe that was probably one of the truest statements I ever heard.

Whatever you're looking for is also looking for you. Every success has a seed—but you must give that seed the time that it needs to mature. You should fill your days with good habits and serve before becoming a leader. Shut out the negative situations and stop complaining about your current conditions. You must engage in consistent action. Things don't always happen when we would like them to—life is a movie—not an episode.

Nurture your skills and be sure to water those talents by refining your gift. If anyone tells you that the process of winning is easy, then you'd better run the other way. Growth takes time, patience and perseverance. How much faith do you have? It's easy to start a business venture, school, a relationship, or a fitness journey. But you'll get to the point when no one's cheering and you're the only person out there. That's when you'll begin to doubt yourself. It's called the growing process—don't stunt your growth by listening to the negative thoughts and criticisms of the world. Stay the course—don't give up and prepare to reap life's harvest.

This brings me to a heroic story of a kid named Keyone Docher. He's one of the main reasons for me writing this book. Keyone was diagnosed with terminal cancer of the nasal cavity at a very young age. In 2001 when his parents announced this to everyone in the family—we were devastated. But to our surprise, six months later he was in remission and beat cancer. Upon leaving St. Jude—he was granted one wish by the make a wish foundation. All he wanted was an all-white piano and that's just what they presented him with. That piano gave him a new passion and a new obstacle to conquer.

Keyone dealt with the side effects of cancer—such as respiratory problems, trouble eating and even slight hearing loss. It didn't bother him one bit, or at least that's how he made it appear. He never complained about anything, no matter how much discomfort he felt. Day-by-day he would call everyone in the room to hear him play some of his favorite songs on his new piano. Each time he got better and better—until one day his music teacher Mrs. Weeks agreed to provide him with piano lessons.

Keyone became a master pianist, a great vocalist and a one of a kind conductor. He went on to finish high school—impact thousands with his gift of music and received a degree from Mississippi State University at the age of 21 years old. Keyone did more in twenty-one years, than most people do in their entire lives.

He's been an inspiration to me since he was a young kid, I remember how passionate he was about his older brother and I playing football. He was always at our games yelling louder than everyone else and was our biggest supporter. A few of his favorite past times were hunting, fishing and horseback riding.

How is it that a young kid with so many obstacles stacked against him—was able to go on to lead a full life? I believe it's because he was a born winner—no obstacle was ever going to be too big for him to achieve. Winners fight—they never give-up; even when things seem impossible—they find a way. Charkelcy "Keyone" Docher, passed away at the tender age of 21 years old—due to breathing complications. His legacy of gratitude, inspiration and perseverance will live on forever.

I'm honored to have had the privilege of having him as a cousin and friend. Keyone was the definition of living a winning life. I would like to thank my Aunt Tammy, Uncle Charles and his older brother Quartez.—for allowing me to share a piece of his amazing story to the world.

Again, I ask. What's preventing you from being the best you possible? What's preventing you from having the career, family and living the life that you deserve? We only have a select amount of days here on earth—then we move on to a greater place. How will you choose to live the days that you have left here? Will you let those days pass by like a cruise ship on the Ocean? Or will you reach out and grab what's yours?

Don't sit back and wait for things to happen—be the cause for the things that are happening. At the end of the day—this is your life; I urge you to stop compromising on the non-negotiable aspects of your life and start confiscating all of the things that this world has to offer. Just remember that actions don't just speak louder than words—They Scream!

"Confidence is self inflicted."
— *TRANSLEE*

CONFIDENCE IS A CHOICE

Let's face it when we were children, no one ever told us that becoming an adult would be hard at all. We believed growing up meant freedom to go and do anything that we wanted to and never have to answer to a single person. Sounds great right? Wrong! Adults don't get many pats on the back, or good jobs—life's not easy at all. It's filled with many beautiful majestic mountains and deep valleys.

The crazy thing is—those same beautiful mountains, are the very things that create the dark valleys and life is no different. There's no golden paved road for you to walk down—no magic tree with hundred dollar bills as leaves, no cure all health pill, or vaccine that cures cancer, heart attacks, strokes, or any terminal illness as of yet.

With that said—I believe that we as human beings must equip ourselves for the journey ahead. Would you go on an extended trip without packing for it? Then you should prepare for life's journey in the same manner. You must be strong internally and externally to handle life—or life will handle you. By reading this book, you're already ahead of the average person—most people don't even try to get better in life. Instead, they simply drift away like a sailboat on the windy sea of life with no captain at the helm. You took the time to read a book, that if applied, could help send your life into a new direction.

Let's be clear, don't expect to read "Win at Life" and wake up in the morning wealthy, healthy and worry-free. Realistically—you wouldn't plant an acorn seed, water it and the next day see a fully-grown oak tree. It takes time, patience and most of all hard work. You must be willing to do and say the things that others fear. Why? Because you're different, you're one of a kind. Other people's opinions of you should only drive you harder and push you beyond your limits.

Don't injure your self-confidence by talking down on yourself. Your best friend—as well as your worst enemy, lives inside of your head. Negative self-talk can be the difference between you flying, or failing. Many people live a quiet life of desperation, solely because they lack the self-confidence to take their situation and lives to the next level.

I struggled with this area for quite some time. It wasn't until I began to speak up for myself that my self-confidence began to grow. I can recall people calling me, asking for favors many times. I would never turn them away—even if I didn't have time, or money, I would still do whatever it was they needed me to do. It was all because I didn't understand how to say no. This simple word "no" can cause you to grow exponentially as a person. It forces you to become a lion instead of a sheep.

Lions stand up for themselves and have a strong determination to do the things that they set their minds too and no one—I mean no one—can deter them. Meanwhile—the sheep are accustomed to following, taking orders, having doubts within themselves and hardly ever take action without being led to do so.

There was a moment in college when I played football at The University of North Alabama under Coach Mark Hudspeth. Coach Hud was an ex-military guy that was stern, but fair to all of his players. He only wanted the best from each of us.

It was early morning—the sun peeked through my bedroom blinds and touched my face. Awakened by the light—I noticed that my alarm clock was off due to the storm during the night. My roommate Dustin and I woke up late for "Mat Room" aka spring training. Training started at 5:00 am—anyone that knew coach, was well aware that his motto was: "To be early is to be on-time and to be on-time is to be late." And beyond late were Dustin and me. We rushed to the gym only to be greeted by a locked door. We walked away with our hearts in our stomach's just knowing that coach was going to punish us beyond anything fathomable.

Later that afternoon, coach called us into his office and asked why we were late that morning? We knew that some fly by night generic excuse wouldn't cut it with him. He could see right through the lies—gaze at the truth and just wait for you to tell him and that's what we did. "We have no excuse Coach" we exclaimed, nodding his head he replied, "I can respect that, just meet me on the football field at 5:00 am sharp tomorrow!" "Yes sir," we said leaving his office dreading the next morning.

Dustin woke up at about 4:00 am that morning and I quickly jumped to my feet soon after—thinking that it was 4:00 pm (we've all done that a time or two). We arrived at the field dressed in our workout attire. It rained the night before, so the football field was moist with a dense fog covering it. The coach said, "all you have to do is run ten one hundred yard sprints." Just as I began to get excited (as if I would get off easy) he said "oh—by the way—you must perform an all out face first dive onto the mud soaked ground every ten yards," I think my heart skipped a few beats.

Dustin looked at me with that "let's get it" look in his eyes. As it began to rain lightly—the whistle blew and we took off full speed, diving into the fog as if it were a pillow-top mattress on the ground. It was the eighth one-hundred yard sprint that my legs gave out. The only thing that I could hear, was Dustin's voice saying "Don't Quit, don't Stop." It was like an annoying song stuck in my head that I couldn't get out, but I kept pushing and kept grinding. Mud filled my face and determination filled my heart.

After getting to the last ten yards, I dove so high that it felt as if I were moving in slow motion. It seemed as if I was in the air for minutes, hours, even days, then I landed on that goal line—Dustin said, "I knew you could do it." Sometimes you have to believe in someone else's belief in you until you're confident enough to believe in yourself.

What is the one thing in your life that you need help conquering? Is it a relationship—a new position at work, or some unforeseen event that has unexpectedly happened in your life? Whatever the case may be—you have to have rhino skin and the heart of a champion. The reason I say that you must have rhino skin is because they have some of the toughest skin on earth—which makes it hard for its predators to penetrate.

With all of the things that your haters are going to say—you're going to need some tough skin so that the words and actions of those haters don't bother you one bit. You'll also have to have the heart of a champion to keep pushing forward toward your goals and never deviate from the course. Just as the section reads—confidence is a choice—so choose to step into the person that you were born to be.

5 KEYS TO GAINING SELF-CONFIDENCE

1. **THINK LIKE A STARTER.** I never got onto the field when I thought like a benchwarmer and the same applies to you and your life—think and act the way you want to be perceived.

2. **SPEAK UP.** Be the icebreaker—don't wait for everyone to speak to you. Although actions speak louder than words, I suggest that you learn to get a strong backbone and speak with the confidence of a "LEADER".

3. **CERTAINTY.** When you're absolutely certain about something—you do it with no hesitation. Make sure that what you say and do match, this is one of the most important keys.

4. **TAKE CHARGE.** Don't get caught up in playing the blame game—you'll never win. Accept responsibility.

5. **EXECUTE.** Fear is an illusion; Action is reality. The only thing stopping you from winning is you. Stop watching from the sidelines and get into the game.

"Winning is about struggle, effort, optimism and never giving up."
— *Amby Burfoot*

ON A WINNING STREAK

AFTER HIGH SCHOOL, I received a football scholarship to play at a small local college near my hometown. When the season started, everyone had high hopes for us, due to the team winning a championship just two years prior. We had a great group of guys and every position was talented.

Somehow we only won two games the entire year. I wasn't accustomed to that—the feeling of not winning and having to accept defeat seemed to haunt me—day in and day out. The coaching staff wasn't organized—practices were cut short and many of the athletes couldn't get along with each other to save their lives.

There's no wonder why we only won two games that year. There was no winning formula in place—no team-driven mission and no passion in the locker room.

After two years of only a handful of wins, I was fortunate enough to receive another scholarship and transferred to The University of North Alabama for my junior & senior years of college. The coach at the time was Mark Hudspeth. He offered me a full scholarship to play football for the University and I gladly accepted.

That would be the beginning of a great season that year. The team was coming off of multiple double-digit winning seasons and a conference championship the year prior. Coach assured me that the pieces of the puzzle were coming together and a championship pedigree was in place. "If we don't win a championship this year, it'll only be because you guys didn't want it bad enough," he said. As I looked at the team—I noticed that we had some guys that should've been playing at major universities and we had the talent to win it all.

The coaching staff had it all together and seemed to be clicking on all cylinders. From the time they recruited me, until the moment I stepped onto the field for the first game—they had a winning formula in place. Everything from planning two-a-day practices to two-minute drills was seamless. I remember asking the coach, why things seemed to run so smoothly? He said, "we've found the recipe for winning." "A recipe for winning... A recipe for winning" I said to myself again. I'd never heard it put like that before. It was as if you could put a tablespoon of passion, a dash of will and a few cups of hard-work and voila—you'd have the winning formula.

As I dug deeper into the statements—I knew that it couldn't be that easy and I was right. It was far from easy; our practices went on for hours and hours. When most schools finished with practices and were sound asleep in their dorms—we were watching game day film and training for our upcoming opponent. All of this was completely voluntary for the players—but we did these sorts of things because it was the culture that we were submerged into.

The winning culture began long before we ever snapped a football in a game, or practice. The culture began with a strong leader that had a vision of what the program would look like, far beyond the present time. A great leader must be willing to respect tradition, but not be afraid to shatter old habits. Great leaders do things in an unconventional way that have a positive effect on the organization. A strong leader is like a good contractor—he plans the project, hires the workers, oversees the work and trains other leaders that can do the same. I believe that our team was great because the coach had a winning system in place—he had the ability to make the entire team and coaching staff, believe in themselves as much as they did the system. The system caused more quality players to want to be apart of the team, let's be honest "winning attracts winners." Whether in sports, business, or relationships this is true.

From that strong pool of talent comes execution of the goal at a very high level and with consistent achievement of an organization's goals, come explosive growth. When a team, or organization is clicking on all cylinders—it's impossible to prevent, or explain how they're growing so fast and winning so much. From the rapid growth comes a shift in the team's mentality—they go from wanting to win sometimes—to expecting to win at all times.

When you have the right system, talent and expectations, then you have the components needed to start and maintain a winning streak. But you must be focused and understand that it won't be easy at all—during the streak—there will be moments that will test your will to win. There will be people that fall off and hop back on the bandwagon—but you must keep your head down and trust your leader's process of getting you to the Promised Land. Winners don't worry about the scoreboard, or the opponent; as long as they give everything they have to accomplishing the goal—they'll be victorious.

THE WINNING CYCLE

PART 4

LEGACY OF A CHAMPION

ALWAYS BEEN A LION

The lion is one of my favorite animals—it's strength, fearlessness and determination makes it the king of the jungle. I always viewed lions in that manner—until one day I visited a local zoo. I noticed many ferocious animals being fed, doing tricks and even being petted. As I made my way to the lion's cage—I couldn't help but notice how weak it looked. Its body was flabby and out of shape, its claws were clipped off and even its roar wasn't as loud as I imagined.

After gazing at the magnificent creature for what seemed like hours—I heard a loud rattling noise growing closer and closer. It was time to eat and the zookeeper was surprisingly in the cage with the lion. I was shocked and afraid of what was about to happen to the keeper. However, the shock soon wore off after I observed the lion eating, what looked to be a giant steak from the keeper's hands. Although cool to watch, this wasn't the animal that I was accustomed to seeing on the discovery channel.

The lions that I remembered would've made lunch of the zookeeper and the giant steak. I had to ask myself—why are these creatures so different if they're essentially the same animal? I stopped and asked the zookeeper—how it was possible for him to interact with the lion on such an intimate level without being harmed? He told me that he raised its mother, father and now him; "what do you mean" I asked? "Well—what we do is, we get them in at birth well before their brains are fully developed and teach them everything we want them to know. That's why they obey me. They know that if I don't feed them—then they won't eat and they love to eat."

A part of me was happy that the lion was always fed and tamed, but another part of me was saddened. I wondered how I would feel locked in a cage, only to jump when someone said jump and eat when someone said eat. You could open the cage of most zoo animals and they'd never attempt to escape. Why? It's because they've been conditioned not to leave the cage. It made me ask myself, "Am I a zoo lion just waiting for others to provide for me—stuck in a daily, weekly, or monthly routine doing things that have little to no meaning? Or am I a wild lion? Strong, Courageous and eating only what he kills."

The wild lion provides for it's family and creates a legacy for the rest of the pride to follow. The reason why I love lions so much is that although it's not the biggest, strongest, or fastest animal in the jungle—it most definitely is the most respected. While one of the largest animals in the jungle is the elephant, whenever it sees the lion it thinks—run. On the other hand—when the lion sees the elephant it doesn't care how big it is—it simply thinks one word—eat. The mentality is what I admire so much. It decides—acts quickly on the decision and carries itself like the king of the jungle—there for it is.

My guess is that you're a wild lion—the king of your own jungle. Everything that you desire to have in this lifetime is yours to have, stop waiting for others to come and give you the things in your life that you were meant to get yourself.

The moral is simple. Don't be like the zoo lion, when the door of life is open—take advantage of the opportunity. Think big and go for it. You'll never be bigger than your negative thoughts. Also, you're capable of going much further than your mental limitations, which are nothing more than past conditioning. Our evolution and DNA gave us the ability to create and do anything that we believe is possible. What are you waiting for? You're a lion!

In life you get out what you put into it.

THE 3 TYPES OF PEOPLE

There was a time when I played football at the collegiate level and there were three different groups of people that were on the team. The first group was what I called "The Reserves." This particular group of individuals was just satisfied to make the team. They didn't care much about playing. Their primary use was helping with practice situations and keeping the team motivated during games. The second group of people were "The Role Players". These individuals had talent—but lacked the elements that could propel them to becoming a starter.

The Third type of person is called "The Starter." This person knows without a shadow of a doubt they are supposed to be on the field. The starter is the person that coaches—as well as the other players—depend on to get the job done, no matter the situation. Each of the three groups possess a different mentality. Reserves don't believe they're good enough to be on the field. They constantly doubt themselves. I've known many talented reserves who never got the opportunity to start, do to their lack of confidence. Role Players make up the majority of people. They don't put in enough work to be a starter—but they're better than the reserves. Finally, the starters have driven personalities and typically become entrepreneurs. Someone who's considered a starter is a trailblazer. Their motto is usually "Less talk, More action."

While playing football at Weir High School—I had a cousin named Charles that was older and more talented than I was at the time. I was one of those people that had talent, but never pushed myself to that "star status" of a player back then.

The coach would give Charles the ball on fourth down and he would score. Charles would go in on the kickoff return team and he would score. It didn't matter where we were on the field—whether we were on offense or defense, he made an impact. It was his senior year of high school football and we became known as the dynamic duo of our division. We were fortunate enough to make it to the state championship game. It was a hard fought game and came down to us being on the one-yard line of the opposing teams end zone. The score was 20-21.

The stage was set—it was overtime and the first team to score was going to win the state championship. All year Charles was the go-to-guy, so there was no doubt in my mind what was about to happen on the one-yard line with the state championship trophy on the line. The crowd was deafeningly loud. The coach called a play and I remember thinking "Yes we're about to win this thing." Everyone knew who was about to score the game-winning touchdown. The opposing team brought all of their guys to the front line so that it was nearly impossible to run through the middle.

As I walked out to my wide-receiver position, I noticed that the quarterback was not handing the ball to Charles who played fullback—needless to say, we were stopped on the one-yard line of the state championship game and the rest is history. The moral of the story is simple. Wherever you are in life, whether you're just happy to be with an organization, or wanting more out your life and career—strive to be the go to person. Be the individual that everyone depends on and looks to in hard times. You have to embrace problem-solving—not run away from it.

If there's one thing that I learned from my cousin Charles, it was that hard work beats talent. He also told me that being average wasn't for us. We did things that others didn't do. While many of our friends were out partying, or doing other things—we were on the football field late at night under the lights, throwing passes—imagining that one day we would be playing at a higher level.

To this day I firmly believe that the relationship I had with my older cousin, formed the work ethic that I have in my present life. That never quit—"will to win by any means necessary mentality" is forever ingrained in me, all because he took me under his wing and allowed me to see the winner I had within myself.

It's all about service, what can you do to help the next person?

PASSING THE BATON

MENTORS ARE ONE ASSET THAT ALL WINNERS are familiar with. A good mentor is like using a modern day GPS to get to a destination, versus an old school map. It can cut the time to get from where you are, to where you want to be in half. Where I'm from, we didn't know anything about having a mentor. It took me awhile to understand the value that a mentor could add to my life—but once I realized it—I made it my obligation to find one.

You may be asking yourself, what exactly is a mentor? In my opinion—a mentor is simply someone who helps you push beyond your expectations and limitations of your current situation. The best investment in life is investing in people—not things.

Nothing succeeds without a great leader and people that help keep the ship afloat. If you observe any great team, company, or organization—they're all a result of great leadership. Before a leader becomes great, another individual must first mentor them. Not in all cases, but most of the time they're a result of another leader. Great leaders don't focus on themselves; they concentrate on building other leaders.

Life, much like business—is about distribution—whether it be power, ideas, philosophies, or products. The wisdom and power of great leaders aren't theirs to keep, but it's meant for them to give away to help the individuals that need it most. With social media on the rise, we have become a culture that wants to gain as many followers as possible. Real leadership is about building other leaders, not followers; they shift the focus from me—to we and think about the generations to come.

The greatest form of leadership is mentoring, because if all of your knowledge, skill, accomplishments and ideas die when you die—then you've failed. People that are insecure will never train others to take the lead. Instead, they'll only try to keep them exactly where they are. They'll never allow an individual "below" them to achieve a higher level of success than they have. This type of person will never make an effective leader, due to their selfish heart and immature mindset. They may make lots of money and accumulate many awards for their personal accomplishments, but they'll never—I repeat NEVER—be recognized as a truly effective leader.

When I think about someone who epitomizes the essence of a great leader—my grandfather Ralph Docher comes to mind. He didn't have some fancy title, or amazing salary. Instead, he specialized in diesel mechanic work his entire life, which meant working 60-70hrs a week to provide for his family. Grandpa recently passed away at the age of 78. While attending his funeral service, there was a moment for the family to share what he meant to them. As if a needle was pricking me in my seat, I promptly stood up and proceeded to tell the individuals in attendance that I viewed my grandfather's life as if it were the chapter in a book.

A book entitled "Docher" (which was his last name). His chapter was so great that the best authors of our time couldn't have written a better version. I then asked, "What will your chapter read?" Who would be willing to pick up a book written about your life?" The crowd sat in silence as if they were reflecting upon their lives. At the time that I said it—it was an emotionally charged challenge to everyone in attendance. But the more I thought about it, the more I began to analyze the meaning of the statements. What will your legacy be? What is it that you will leave your family, that they won't cash in for a quick buck after you leave this earth?

I was never the type that looked up to many people—only my uncle, David Kent Miller. I looked up to him because of his athleticism, dedication to his country and all of the many things that he accomplished throughout his life. He always put others before himself, whether he was on a sports team, in combat as a police officer, or during his service in the military. He was never the self-centered guy that wanted all the glory, but was a person that had a heart of gold and the soul of a servant.

I'll never forget him teaching me to tie my shoes. I couldn't have been any more than four or five years old. As a young child—my feet turned inward so badly that I had to get "Forrest Gump" walking braces on my legs before I could walk straight. I think the term was bowlegged, or pigeon toed. I would constantly trip over my own feet causing me to untie my shoes accidentally.

When I got older—I began going to Uncle Kent for advice about running track. He was an astounding track runner and was fortunate enough to receive a scholarship to run for Jackson Sate University. I wanted to be great at track and began asking him questions ranging from how to start off, too how to breathe while running. He gave me some great advice and I was successful in the relay races that I competed in, "Whatever you do don't drop the baton" he said. He told me that the most important part of a relay race wasn't running, "it's not?" I said. It's passing the baton he told me. The reason why is because if you drop it—then you and your entire team will be disqualified from the race.

He made me practice more on handing off the baton than I did running. For those that don't know—in a relay race there are four runners. When one runner is passing the baton, the other person never looks back—but reaches his hand back, expecting the baton. How many people are looking for you to pass the baton, but you're trying to run the entire race by yourself? Or how many of you have your arm back waiting for someone to pass it to you?

There are some things in life that those closest to you are not going to understand until you pass the baton.

There are some situations that they won't know how to deal with until you pass the baton. When you pass it—not just one person wins, but everyone wins. Developing other people must be at the forefront of any winning team, or organization.

Mentors help you cut down on your failure rate, they give you an unfair advantage over anyone in direct competition with you who doesn't have one. Think about it—how long would it have taken you to learn how to drive a car if no one ever taught you how to do it? How long would it have taken you to discover how to write if no one ever guided you in writing?

If you want to do anything entrepreneurial, or business-related and perform at a very high level—it's hard to do without having a mentor to guide you along the way. It would be very hard for someone who hit the lottery to teach you how to make money because they don't know how—they didn't extract the lessons from the process of organically making money. On the other hand, someone who started with nothing and worked their way towards "success"—can show and tell you how they did it, as well as, give you advice on how you can do the same.

Be picky with the person who you choose as a mentor—they should have the things that you desire and affect you and other individuals in a positive way. Sit down and ask yourself, what will the chapters of your life read? Adjust them accordingly to make them better. Remember that someday the mentee becomes the mentor—always be willing to help other young men and women reach their desired goals by passing the baton.

*Teachers are the foundation
of the people.*

THE TEACHER EFFECT

SOME PEOPLE THAT YOU MEET, will have an immediate impact on your life. That person for me was a teacher named Ms. Aldridge—she was my fourth-grade teacher. Ms. Aldridge stood barely five foot tall, had a caramel skin complexion, with a small button nose. I was easily the worst behaved kid in the entire fourth-grade class. I never paid attention and was always getting into trouble.

There would even be times that I would sneak off of the school grounds when we had recess, just because I could—I didn't care. Most of the time I was late for school because my mother had to take my youngest brother to daycare, my middle brother to his school and I would be the last to get to class many times. My mother worked two jobs at the time and was raising us by herself, so I never got into trouble about being late. Ms. Aldridge and my mother would always talk to me and beg me to do things right, they would even punish me when I did things wrong—but that never helped me. I honestly didn't care at all. I felt like no one could tell me anything and I would never listen to anyone.

I'll never forget the time when Ms. Aldridge called my mother to the school because I was in trouble yet again. Most of the grades on my report card were F's and D's. I can recall walking into the office for a parent-teacher meeting and me not even being afraid or nervous.

My mother and Ms. Aldridge began to talk—they both sat across from me, with pain in their faces because they wanted me to do better. My mother sat on the left and Ms. Aldridge sat to the right of me. A single tear rolled down Ms. Aldridge's left cheek. That teardrop carried within it hurt, pain and the longing for a young man to change his ways. They begged me to change and I shrugged it off as if the whole conversation didn't matter to me. Needless to say—I never changed that year. At the end of the school year when final report cards came out—I noticed my friends all opening their report cards.

One-by-one, each of them rejoiced with excitement—when it was time for me to open mine, I slowly opened it in hopes of a miracle. The report card had two F's and three D's—it finally hit me that my friends were advancing on and I was forced to stay back. That hurt me more than anything. I began to pay attention and wonder how things could become if I adopted a winning attitude.

After failing the fourth grade and being humbled by the embarrassment of not passing on to the fifth. We moved to Fort Drum, (a small army base in upstate New York near Syracuse). This was a new experience for me. All I'd ever known was the south, so to move up north where the weather was bone-chilling cold and the people sounded like they were from another planet, was a whole new experience for me. Their words were so precise and their dialect was so different—I never heard anything like it in my life.

I can recall starting at my new school and me telling the counselor that I didn't belong in the fourth grade. At first, she laughed as if it were a joke. After being in the fourth grade for only a few weeks and being seemingly more advanced than the other students—the counselor and teacher insisted that I take an advancement test. The exam would test my skill level and place me in the grade that fit my level. After taking that test, the counselor said: "You belong in the sixth grade." You see, I was never illiterate or not smart enough, I just always had a big imagination that caused me to lose focus at times. Ms. Aldridge lit a fire under me in the fourth grade that still burns even to this day.

I'm not sure where Ms. Aldridge is—but if I ever see her again, I'll thank her from the bottom of my heart for the way that she cared about a young kid that was raised primarily by a single teenage parent.

How many of you have a teacher, coach, or family member that has had a serious impact on your life and has pushed you beyond the person that you ever thought you could be? Your life is merely a collection of people and events—by not settling for mediocrity you return the favor to all of those that have invested in you along your journey to winning at life.

Dwaeuntre Davis

STORY OF A TRUE CHAMPION

WHAT IF I TOLD YOU that a 19-year-old kid was shot and killed for doing nothing wrong at all. Most of you would say, "Yeah that happens a lot lately." But what if I told you that the 19-year-old kid was your son, friend, or family member? That feels a bit different, doesn't it? Well on April 25, 2005 that's exactly what we had to call and tell my best friend D.D. Davis's parents.

I was a sophomore cornerback and D.D. was a freshman wide receiver on the football team. He was a short guy—but was always the fastest person on the football field.

My first couple of years in college, I stayed to myself—I didn't trust many people being around me like that. But the short light-skinned kid from Louisiana would always come into my dorm room, joking and playing as only he could. I had no choice but to grow close to him; I constantly joked with D.D. that he only hung out with me because I was the teams barber and he wanted free haircuts. His reply was always, "It worked didn't it?" I guess it did work because he became like a younger brother to me.

It was the end of spring—for us football players, that meant practice was almost over and parties were about to begin. This particular night on campus, was one of the biggest parties of the year. It was a time to celebrate being finished with finals and getting ready for summer vacation.

While getting dressed to go to the party, I received an unusual phone call from my father who lived about thirty minutes away at the time. He said, "Hey son, I bought some groceries for you and I want you to come to the house to get them today. I was caught off-guard, anytime I ever needed groceries before, I'd go pick them up at the store myself.

Still a bit confused I said, not tonight Pops I'm going to this party, it's the last one of the semester, I explained. He kept insisting until I finally gave in.

As I made it to my father's house, I received a phone call; it was my roommate Eric. "They shot him—he was just standing there," he said. I said who shot who? (D.D.) they shot D.D. I knew it wasn't a joke, I could hear the pain in Eric's voice.

Pops wouldn't let me leave his house that night out of fear that we would retaliate. That night I cried so much that my soul hurt, I lost my brother and best friend. Had it not been for my father calling me to pick up the groceries, I would've been right next to D.D.

Some parts of me wish I would've been there to save him, but as my grandpa always said, "When it's your time, it's your time." He was right; it wasn't my time. I had to write this book for you and fulfill my obligation of serving the world one person at a time.

I wrote this section, not for pity towards D.D.'s family or myself. I wrote this because one day someone in your family is going to receive a phone call saying that you are no longer with us. Today is all you have, make the most of it—as cliché as that sounds.

If you ever decide to dream, dream so big that it scares you. If you ever decide to speak, be sure that you say something that captivates someone's heart. And if you ever decide to win at something, choose to WIN AT LIFE!

ABOUT THE AUTHOR

Keldrick "KD" Docher is a writer, visionary and aspiring entrepreneur. Coming from humble beginnings he understands the true meaning of hard work and commitment. Born into a family of athletes he's won multiple championships on many different levels in his sports and business career, so who better to talk about the subject than someone who's actually been there and done it?

Being the first person of his immediate family to attend college, he faced and overcame many issues. He received a full scholarship in football; the goal for him was to make it to the professional level until he lost passion for the game he loved. Soon after college he took his competitive nature from the football field to the corporate level and landed a job with a 14 billion dollar company. KD is passionate about uplifting individuals that are in need. He believes that each person on this earth serves a purpose and has a unique gift, but it's up to each person to discover it. KD currently resides in Atlanta, Georgia where he aims to be of continued service to humanity.

Made in the USA
Columbia, SC
05 April 2018